WITHOUT FUTURE

Map of Syria

WITHOUT FUTURE

The Plight of Syrian Jewry

Saul S. Friedman

PRAEGER

New York
Westport, Connecticut
London

Library of Congress Cataloging-in-Publication Data

Friedman, Saul S.
    Without future : the plight of Syrian Jewry / Saul S. Friedman.
      p. cm.
    Bibliography: p.
    Includes index.
    ISBN 0–275–93313–X (lib. bdg. : alk. paper)
    1. Jews—Syria—Persecutions. 2. Syria—Ethnic relations.
  I. Title.
    DS135.S95F75 1989
    956.91′004924—dc19   89–3769

British Library Cataloguing in Publication Data is available.

Library of Congress Catalog Card Number: 89–3769
ISBN: 0–275–93313–X

First published in 1989

Praeger Publishers
One Madison Avenue, New York, NY 10010

Printed in the United States of America

The paper used in this book complies with the
Permanent Paper Standard issued by the National
Information Standards Organization (Z39.48–1984).

10 9 8 7 6 5 4 3 2 1

For Raphaela

Contents

Preface

People ask why I became involved with the plight of Syrian Jewry, why an Ashkenazic Jew whose grandparents came from Poland invited an Iraqi Jew to speak at a Yom ha-Shoah program in Youngstown in 1970. My response is that I am one of those cantankerous souls who has rebuked American Jews who were living during the Holocaust. In *No Haven for the Oppressed* (Wayne State 1973), in the Goldberg Commission Report (Holmes and Meier 1985), and in numerous forums around the country, I have said repeatedly that American Jews did not do enough to help their brethren when Hitler ruled Europe. At times, critics have misquoted me, saying I have charged American Jews with doing nothing, and taunting that my own criticisms have been framed from forty years of hindsight.

I am not, however, a *weinweiber* (professional weeper). It gives me no solace to light candles for the six million murdered in the Holocaust. It is not sufficient to remember. If the Holocaust is to have any meaning, then people must not only remember, they must teach, learn, and translate those lessons into action.

When I first began to teach Middle East history more than twenty years ago, I was struck by parallels between the treatment of Jews in Europe and in Arab lands. More specifically, I was disturbed by the way that isolated Jewish communities were being brutalized in a fashion reminiscent of prewar Nazi Germany. Apparently, I was not alone in this perception. Appearing before an international conference organized by the American Jewish Committee in Paris in 1986, Nazi-hunter Beate Klarsfeld declared:

Jews are the scapegoats for all the anti-Israel feeling in the Middle East. The various Lebanese groups are fighting each other, but they express their hatred of Israel by kidnapping and killing the few Jews left. They are behaving just like the Nazis during World War II—They are killing Jews just because they are Jews. There is no government to defend them.[1]

A similar observation was offered ten years earlier by Itzhak Dror, a teenage Jew from Damascus who was imprisoned and tortured for six months for the crime of attempting to escape from Syria. When he finally managed to reach Israel, Itzhak enrolled in a variety of courses, one of which was about the Holocaust. As an assignment, his instructor asked the class to read the textbook and write their impressions of what life was like under Nazi rule. Itzhak received an "A" and several compliments on his paper, to which he replied, "I did not read the text. I wrote about life in Syria instead."[2]

Until now, concern for the welfare of Jews remaining in Syria has prevented their story from being told. A number of rabbis, scholars, and businessmen from Tel Aviv to Brooklyn believe the time is ripe to speak out and apply pressure, the same kind of publicity that has contributed to the renewed trickle of Jewish emigrés from the Soviet Union. As Arlette Adler of Haifa University's Bridging the Gap Program commented, "It is very important. There are so many people working on *Shoah* [Holocaust], but few dealing with these problems. So much information is being lost. We must develop a sense of education, history, among the Syrian Jews and others so this part of our history will not be lost."[3]

The trick is to tell the tale without jeopardizing the refugees or their families or friends. For that reason, I have changed the names of all principals. The reader will note another limitation to this oral testament: there is no discussion of specific escape routes. During the Holocaust, Danish Jews fleeing to nearby Sweden hid in railroad flatcars ferried across the straits to Malmö and Helsingborg. When amused Swedish newspapers published the story, the Nazis halted the boat trains and shut down this escape route.

I have not attempted to draw great sociological lessons or, as some have suggested, to develop patterns of survival and resistance. This is the story of people, individuals who have struggled, with little external support, against merciless persecution. The story is incomplete, even sketchy at this time. As long as there are Jews in Syria, it would be dangerous to reveal details of diplomatic interventions or escape. For that we will have to wait, as one rescuer has said, "until every last Jew is out of Syria." And that may never happen.

I have no illusions about the effect this book may have, other than to let the Jews of Syria know that others care and are working to help. In my researches, I have been assisted by many individuals. In Israel, they include Miriam Meyouchas and her Sephardic Women's Association; Dr. Avraham Chaim of Hebrew University's Misgav Yerushalayim Institute; David Sitton; Herzlia Lokay and Arlette Adler; Moishe Cohen and Ora Schweitzer of the World Organization of Jews from Arab Countries; and, Simona Frankel of the Foreign Office. In New York, my appreciation goes to Dr. George Gruen of the American Jewish Committee; Sherry Hyman of the Joint Distribution Committee; Mr. Stephen Shalom;

workers of Sephardic *Bikur Holim;* and, the staff of Congressman Stephen Solarz. Closer to home, I want to thank Dean Bernard Yozwiak of Youngstown State University's College of Arts and Sciences who was solely responsible for the administrative leave, in 1986, that made my trip to the Middle East possible and to YSU students Deanna Beachley, Tim Clifton, Aziz Alhadi, and Abeer Jadallah, the latter two who prove that Jews and Arabs can work together for humanity.

Finally, a word of appreciation to the volunteers of the National Task Force for Syrian Jews of the Canadian Jewish Congress and deceased leaders of Toronto's Jewish community (Dr. Ronald Feld and Kayla Armel) who made the cause of Syrian *peletim* (refugees) their own. This book could not have been undertaken without their assistance or the herculean efforts of one woman, Judy Feld Carr. For nearly twenty years, virtually alone, she has pleaded the case of this vulnerable minority in the halls of Canadian government, before international conferences, with detached Israeli foreign officers, on college campuses, and in synagogues. No one has done more to preserve the dignity of Syrian Jews or to encourage their relief. For the Jews living in the absorption centers of Jerusalem or apartments in Ocean Parkway, she is an adopted sister, a godmother. For those still trapped in the Haret el-Yahud of Damascus, she is "Mrs. Judy," their hope and lifeline to a free world. We all owe her an unrepayable debt of gratitude for reminding us *"vos vetzayn mit Reb Yisroel vetzayn mit Klal Yisroel* [what happens to an individual Jew is felt by all Jews].''

1

The Myth of Islamic Toleration

Ten years ago, I was asked to deliver a speech on the status of Jews in Arab lands before a group of Hillel students at Ohio State University. When the talk was over, an individual identifying himself as the Imam of a mosque in Columbus came up and informed me that I was incorrect. Anti-Semitism was a thing unknown to the Middle East, a region that had welcomed Jews when they were oppressed by Christian Europeans. Historically, Jews and Arabs lived in Semitic fraternity until the onset of Herzlian Zionism at the end of the nineteenth century. Arabs have been made to pay for the horrors of the Holocaust, a catastrophe that could not have happened in the Islamic world because the Quran contains "not a single word which is antagonistic toward Jews." It was a familiar litany, one sounded repeatedly in the principal texts on the Middle East, one that is inaccurate and dangerous, because it glosses over the pain that victims of bigotry have endured.[1]

So long as the *ahl al-kitab* (People of the Book) paid their *jizyah* (poll tax) commanded by Muhammad, they were not to be disturbed in the practice of their religion. The way even seemed open for them to salvation, as the Quran stipulates, "Those who attend to their prayers and pay the alms tax and have faith in Allah and the Last Day—these shall be richly rewarded" (Sura of Women 4:162; Table 5:66).[2] Officially, Jews and Christians were *dhimmi* (protected people), fellow monotheists who were to be tolerated by the Arabs.

The term "toleration" does not of itself connote affection or respect, rather a willingness to abide, however reluctantly, the existence of something or some group that may be personally distasteful (e.g., nonsmokers tolerating smokers). Toleration in the Islamic world never implied equality. In the stratified world

of the Middle East, the People of the Book (Christians as well as Jews) were to
be counted above the level of pagans, but significantly below that of true believers. As misguided souls who might be consigned to the hellfire, they were
to suffer "lighter punishment" in this world (Adoration 32:21).

The threat of persecution was more serious and immediate for Jews. Although
Muslims did slaughter Christians, and Christians retaliated in kind, a balance of
terror operated between the two peoples, affording their brethren at least the
illusion of immunity wherever they lived. Unlike Christians, Jews had no great
empires (such as Rome, Byzantium, Axum, and the Carolingians) posing as
their protectors. Moreover, three Jewish tribes that resided in Medina (the Qay-
nuka, an-Nadir, and Qurayzah) had especially provoked Muhammad when they
ridiculed and rejected the Prophet's conversionary overtures. For that, they were
cursed and purged from the city.

The Quran does not limit its contempt for Jews to the destruction of Jewish
tribes in Hejaz. The sacred text of Islam allows that Allah guided the Israelites
across the Red Sea and settled them in a blessed land (Jonah 10:90). He also
gave the Scriptures, "bestowed on them wisdom and prophethood" (Kneeling
45:16), free from evil motives (Houd 11:110). Israelites who understood the true
nature of the good book would participate in the blessings of paradise (The Ant
27:76). Unfortunately, these were few, because Jews had wronged themselves
(Bee 16:118) by losing faith (Heights 7:168) and breaking the covenant (Table
5:13). Sounding much like an ante-Nicaean polemic, the Quran contends that
the Jews are a nation that has "passed away" (Cow 2:134, 141). Twice God
sent his instruments (the Assyrians and Romans) to punish this perverse people
(Night Journey 17:4–5), and their dispersal over the face of the earth is proof
of his rejection (Heights 7:168). For the arrogant Jews who still claim to be his
chosen people, the Quran instructs, "Say to the Jews: If your claim be true that
of all men you alone are Allah's friends, then you should wish for death" (Friday,
or Day of Congregation 62:6).

The Quran contains an impressive indictment of the Jews' sins. Apart from
breaking the covenant, they "denied the revelations of Allah and killed their
prophets unjustly" (Women 4:155). Abuse of prophets is a consistent theme.
In the Sura of the Cow, Jews are asked, "Why did you kill the prophets of
Allah if you are true believers?" (Cow 2:91). Jews are chastised for plotting
against Jesus (Imrams 3:55; Women 4:157). Instead of revering Muhammad,
whom they ridicule as *Ra'ina* (the evil one) (Cow 2:104; Women 4:46), these
"perverse" creatures say Ezra is the messiah and they worship rabbis who
defraud men of their possessions (Repentance 9:30).

Mentioned briefly as hypocrites and unbelievers in the Sura of Exile (59:11),
Jews are especially vilified in Medinan chapters of the Quran. In a long diatribe
in the Sura of the Cow, where they are typified as an "envious" people (2:109)
whose hearts are "hard as rock" (2:74), Jews are accused of confounding the
truth (2:42), deliberately perverting scripture (2:75), and telling lies (2:78).
Illiterate, senseless people of little faith (2:89), they engage in vague and wishful

fancies (2:111). Shame and misery have been stamped on them for their transgressions (2:62), which include usury (2:275), breaking the Sabbath (2:65), sorcery (2:102), hedonism (2:95), and idol worship (2:53).

Idol worship comes up again in connection with false gods in the Sura of Women (4:51). Here Jews are faulted for a chain of "iniquities"—their lack of faith, taking words out of context, disobedience and distortion (4:45), their "monstrous falsehoods" (4:156), usury, and cheating (4:160). The charge of cheating is prominently featured in Imrams where most Jews are accused of being "evildoers" (3:111) who, deceived by their own lies (3:224), try to "debar believers from the path of Allah and seek to make it crooked" (3:99). Jews mislead (3:69), confound the truth (3:71), twist tongues (3:79), and say, "We are not bound to keep faith with Gentiles" (3:75). Believers are advised by the Sura of the Table not to take these clannish people as their friends (5:51). "The most implacable of men in their enmity to the faithful" (Table 5:82), Jews are blind and deaf to the truth (5:71). What they have not forgotten, they have perverted (5:13). Warns the Sura of She Who Pleaded (58:14–19):

Do you see those that have befriended a people [the Jews] with whom Allah is angry? They belong neither to you nor to them. They knowingly swear to falsehoods. Allah has prepared for them a grievous scourge. Evil indeed is that which they have done.

They use their faith as a disguise and debar others from the path of Allah. A shameful scourge awaits them.

Neither their wealth nor their children shall in the least protect them from Allah. They are the heirs of Hell and there they shall abide forever.

On the day when Allah restores them all to life, they will swear to Him as they now swear to you, thinking that their oaths will help them. Surely they are liars all.

Satan has gained possession of them and caused them to forget Allah's warning. They are the confederates of Satan; Satan's confederates shall assuredly be lost.

Here, at last, is the ultimate sin of the Jews—they are among the devil's minions (see also Women 4:60). Cursed by God, their faces will be obliterated (Women 4:47). If they do not accept the true faith, on the day of judgment, they will be made into apes (Women 2:65, Heights 7:166) and burn in the hellfire (Women 4:55). As it is written in the Sura of the Proof, "The unbelievers among the People of the Book and the pagans shall burn for ever in the fire of Hell. They are the vilest of all creatures" (Proof 98:7).

None of the early leaders of Islam disputed these teachings. Of the good Jew al-Zabir, Abu Bekr said, "He will meet his beloved ones again in Hell." Several *hadith* (sayings attributed to Muhammad) established the prophet's hostility toward Jews. Their children might be forcibly converted because "everyone is born in a natural state of religion" (Islam) and only their parents have made them Jews or Christians. Jews were a perverse people who were not to be treated kindly in this world. Muhammad is supposed to have said, "Verily you will combat against the Jews, so carry through the fight until a stone would say: O Muslim, this is a Jew: come along and smite him down." In a variation on this theme, the Prophet allegedly remarked, "O Muslim Servants of God, there are Jews behind me; come and kill them."[3]

On his deathbed, Muhammad advised that two religions should not coexist in Arabia. Umar, the second caliph, took the prophet at his word, breaking treaties with Jews living north of Medina, driving them from their lands, and assigning their property to warriors. It was also Umar who expelled Jews from Jerusalem and Tiberias, appropriated their synagogues, and instituted anti-Jewish legislation resembling the jim crow system of the U.S. South.

The so-called Rule of Umar was the operative legal and social code in the Middle East for 1,300 years. For the privilege of a precarious existence under Islam, Jews over the age of fifteen had to pay not only the degrading *jizyah* (collected at times with an accompanying slap in the face), but also a *kharaj* (land tax) and *ghanimah* (property tax amounting to one-tenth of an individual's income), and contribute girls to a lord's harem. At customs posts, they were to pay double the tariff on Muslim goods. To forestall massacres, special ransoms (*avanies*) were extorted from their communities.[4]

In this system, Jews were viewed as a deceitful, unreliable people. They were not to touch the Quran, lest they mock or falsify Islamic holy writ. They were forbidden to speak of Islam or the Prophet with irreverence. Just such a critique resulted in the execution of Saadia ibn Yusuf, the ninth-century sage oft-cited as an example of how Judaism flowered under Islam. A Jew's word was unacceptable in a court of law and Jews were deemed untrustworthy in administrative posts. Fearing the wrath of Muslim mobs, Moses Maimonides, adviser and personal physician to Saladin, openly practiced Islam. Not so fortunate were Joseph ibn Nagrela, wazir of Granada who was crucified along with 1,500 Jewish families on December 30, 1066; Saad Adduala, adviser to the Ilkhan Argun, whose ambitions prompted widespread massacres in Persia in 1291; Khalifa ben Waqqasa, slain because he became chamberlain to Abu Yakub in 1301; and Aaron ibn Batash, whose appointment as minister led to the extermination of Fez Jewry in 1465.[5]

Accorded special status as a protected religious group, Jews were not to proselytize or do anything else that might disturb their Muslim neighbors. The blowing of the ceremonial ram's horn at the New Year was to be done quietly. So, too, the chanting of the *kaddish* over the dead. No new synagogues were to be constructed. Those that existed in a town were to be smaller than mosques. If they fell into disrepair or were destroyed by fire, vandalism, or natural calamity, they were not to be rebuilt. According to Maurice Roumani, Muslim rulers in Egypt, Iraq, and Syria routinely extorted great sums from their Jewish subjects, then issued decrees ordering the destruction of Jewish institutions.[6]

Jews were not to approach Muslim shrines, including, for example, the tombs of Ezekiel in Mesopotamia or Samuel near Jerusalem, which had been sacred to the Jewish people for more than a millennium before the arrival of Arab warriors. Into the twentieth century, the punishment for any Jew who passed beyond the eighth step leading up and into the sanctuary of the Patriarchs (Abraham, Isaac, and Jacob) in Hebron was death.[7] Jewish cemeteries were to be distinguished by flat grave markers, which contrasted with the miniature cenotaphs favored by Muslims. And even here, whether the cemetery was located in Marrakesh or Nablus, the Jews were not to be free from curses, spit in their face, or other harassment.

Devoid of honor, Jews could not make use of anything—signet rings, cummerbunds, canes, sedan chairs—that symbolized nobility. In an age when a man's worth was gauged by his accomplishments on the battlefield, Jews were barred from the military. Nevertheless, they still had to pay a special tax for this legally imposed exemption. Jews were not to ride horses or mules, only donkeys, and then without saddles. Anything else might prompt a riot among the Arab populace. A U.S. intelligence report from San'a, Yemen, dated May 29, 1946, related how a mob nearly killed an American soldier whose offense was that he offered a ride in a jeep to a Jewish woman and her child.[8]

Wherever Jews traveled, their inferiority was clearly established. In their places of business, they were to rise in the presence of a Muslim. On the streets, they were to dismount and inquire of the Muslim's "exalted health." When passing a Muslim, Jews were to take the left, or what was traditionally regarded as the unclean side. In some communities, Jews were not permitted to be on the same streets as Muslims. In Tunisia, they were to fall on their knees when they passed the Casbah (central fort). Into this century, in parts of Iran, Jews were not to walk in the rain, for fear they might contaminate the water. Jews were barred from making use of the very public facilities—city latrines and bathhouses—that they were often forced to clean. It was not unusual for them to be summoned from Yom Kippur services to perform such degrading maintenance work. If they came in contact with a Shiite Muslim's eating utensils, the objects might have to be destroyed.[9] Any male Jew who touched, married, or had sex with a Muslim woman might forfeit his life and property. The same was true for a Jew who, having been insulted or assaulted, attempted self-defense.

To minimize contact with untouchable Jews, the Arab world invented the Jewish badge, some form of apparel to stigmatize the Jews. Five centuries before the *rouelle* (circular badge) was introduced in Europe by Pope Innocent III, Umar decreed that Jews must wear a distinctive sash known as the *zunnar* (really a piece of rope) around their midsections along with a piece of yellow cloth on their robes. In 807, the fabled monarch Harun al-Rashid enforced the rule throughout his empire. Fifty years later, al-Mutawwakil compelled Jews to wear yellow scarves (the same color that was employed by the Nazis in the ghettos and extermination camps of Europe) along with pointed skullcaps resembling the headgear of wizards or witches. In virtually every sector of the Islamic world, Jews were forbidden to wear colorful garb. In Almohade Spain (1130–1212), Sultan Yakub al-Mansur ordered Jews to dress in black cloaks with wide sleeves and black, pointed caps. In Algeria, Jews were not permitted to wear shoes with heels or to cover their feet with stockings in the summer. In Morocco, they were not to wear turbans or shoes like those of Moors. In Yemen, Jewish women were required to wear shoes of different colors, one white, one black, connoting ignorance and identifying them as pariahs.[10]

Another inhuman device—the ghetto—also originated in the Islamic world. Nearly a thousand years before Pope Paul IV proclaimed the first official ghetto in Rome, hundreds of years before informal *Juderias* and *Judengassen* sprang up in Western European cities, the Rule of Umar compelled Jews to live in special quarters known as *haras* or *mellahs*. Generally the most dilapidated section of a city, the Arab ghetto was unlit and sealed off at night.[11] Rags fluttered over the houses as an additional indication that the residents were Jews. Disease and overcrowding were common. As late as 1950, most of the Jewish children in Casablanca, Tunis, and Fez (where population densities exceeded 1,000 per square acre) suffered from malnutrition, intestinal disorders, tuber-culosis, ringworm, and impetigo.[12] One interesting variation of the "Jew Street" developed in parts of the Atlas Mountains and Libya. Until the founding of the state of Israel, some Jews in these areas lived like troglodytes (cave dwellers). When Muammar al-Qaddafi tried to entice Libyan emigrés back from Israel with an offer of their former domiciles in the mid–1980s, he found no takers.[13]

The attempt to isolate, ridicule, and debase the Jews was carried to an extreme in the reign of Fatimid Caliph al-Hakim in Egypt (966–1021). A self-deluded fanatic who considered himself the redeemer of mankind, al-Hakim maintained that the Jews still worshipped the golden calf, and he required them to wear little images of this animal about their necks. When this humiliation failed to induce conversion to Islam, the monarch decreed they should wear cowbells around their necks. This device also failed, therefore, the caliph ordered the Jews to wear six-pound wooden blocks about their necks. Finally, on Passover in the year 1012, al-Hakim ordered the destruction of the Jewish quarter of Cairo with all its inhabitants.[14]

What happened under al-Hakim was not an isolated incident. Pogroms form a recurring theme in the history of Islam. After causing an initial bloodbath, Idris, the first Fatimid caliph of Morocco (c. 788), established the precedent of demanding oppressive taxes and an annual supply of twenty-four Jewish virgins for his harem. A century later, persecution at the hands of this dynasty prompted many Jews to flee to Spain. In 1032, the conquest of Fez by sons of Afran was accompanied by the murder of 6,000 Jews. The annals of Tlemcen, Algiers, Marrakesh, and Fez tell of burned synagogues, desecrated Torahs, and decap-itated rabbis in the years 1275, 1465, and 1790–1792. The worst atrocities, however, may have taken place between 1143 and 1179 when the Almohades (fundamentalist zealots from the Atlas Mountains) swept across North Africa and into Spain, ravaging academies in Seville, Córdoba, and Lucena. Given the choice between conversion to Islam and death, many Jews followed the counsel of Maimonides who instructed his brethren to circumvent these "bigoted rulers" by becoming false converts to Islam.[15]

In the east, documents from the Cairo *geniza* (a repository of Jewish communal documents) reveal additional persecutions under the successors of al-Hakim. Jews in Alexandria and Cairo were plundered in 1168, 1265, and 1524. Sultan Baybars in the thirteenth century blamed the Jews for having started a plague and subjected them to massacre, extortion, and expulsion. When Egyptian nationalists led by Ahmed Urabi struck for liberty against Brtitish imperialists in the 1880s, their first targets were not military installations, but the Jewish ghettos. Desperately seeking some force that would keep their cause alive at the turn of the century, Egyptian extremists even seized the canard of ritual murder, which also served to spark massacres of Jews in Mashhad, Iran, in 1839, and Damascus in 1840.[16]

In Yemen, Muslim emirs waged a constant struggle against isolated Jewish communities that defiled the holy land. In 1474 and 1679, the Jewish quarter of San'a was subjected to pillage; synagogues were converted to mosques as Zaydi chieftains tried to expel this unwelcome group. In Palestine, the Muslim population rampaged against Jews in 809, in the middle of the fifteenth century, between 1625 and 1627, and again at Safed in 1834–1838. Western scholars may draw on court histories to recount the quaintness of the Middle East, but the reality is that Jews have been brutalized from Shapur to the Barbary States.[17]

The saga of Judah Halevi exemplifies the Jewish dilemma under Islam. One of three sages commonly recited as an example of what George Antonius calls a history "remarkably free from instances of deliberate persecution" (the other two are Saadia and Maimonides), Halevi was the foremost Jewish poet of the twelfth century. Unwilling to bear the bigotry of his native Toledo and having written panegyrics to the city of his heart—Jerusalem—Halevi eventually made his way to Zion. As he knelt in prayer outside the city, a passing Saracen allegedly threw a lance into the back of this Jew who could live in neither Christian Europe nor the Islamic Middle East.[18]

The prevailing wisdom among scholars of Middle Eastern history is to dismiss incidents of Arab racism as aberrational. Cleaving to a crass, but expedient European practice that divorces the message of love and hope in the Gospels from the bloody actions of Christians inspired by anti-Jewish rants in Matthew and John, some scholars argue that it is unfair to interpret the words of the Quran as the *ulema* (teachers) and mobs have done throughout history. In implementing the Rule of Umar, Islam was merely following the lead of a much more cruel Byzantine system (conveniently defunct and lacking defenders these past 500 years).[19] Historians sympathetic to the Jewish plight (Norman Stillman and Bat Ye'or) are sometimes over cautious about pinpointing responsibility for their suffering under Islam. However miserable the Jews may have been, they were, after all, protected by the Rule of Umar. Jews "accepted their enforced humility philosophically. They considered it to be part of the burden of a people in exile, and they adhered punctiliously to the restrictions imposed upon them."[20] Or, as another scholar has recently phrased it, "Jews have developed mechanisms for acting effectively in these matters."[21] As for instances of massacre, plunder, and expulsion in the Middle East, they are episodic, anomalous, and dwarfed by the tragic saga of Jews in Europe.[22]

Such reasoning accounts, in part, for the inability of Western observers to understand the mind-set of Jewish refugees from Arab lands. If Jews were *dhimmi,* protected people, Sephardic Jews ask, from whom, other than Muslims, were they protected? If Islamic society was color-blind and tolerant, why was it necessary for rulers, be they Abbasid caliph or Ottoman sultan, to emulate medieval Popes by issuing *firmans* explaining that Jews must not be attacked as agents of Satan? What is the justification for projecting an antebellum passivity on a people legally barred from defending themselves from attack? And finally, if Islamic society abetted the development of Jewish philosophy, poetry, and wealth, how can one account for the fact that whenever a Jew rose to a position of authority, a pogrom followed?

Such incidents were not of a sporadic nature. Hatred of Jews was a constant that was expressed throughout the Islamic world. The Ottomans who gave the Jews sanctuary following their expulsion from Spain in the fifteenth century did so not from any altruistic impulse, but to enhance their own economic system by the addition of people they referred to as "mangy dogs."[23] Among Egyptians, Edward Lane reported, "It is common to hear an Arab abuse his jaded ass, and after applying to him various opprobrious epithets, end by calling the beast a Jew."[24] In Iraq in 1922, Ahmed Rihani quoted an Arab who refused to go into the Jewish quarter: "Whenever the name of Yahuda is mentioned—Allah curse him—I have to spit."[25] In Palestine, where the friendship between Jews and Arabs has been vaunted, it was common in the twentieth century for Arabs to refer to Jews as *shayatin* (devils), *awlad al-mawt* (children of death), or *siknag* (a corruption of Ashkenazim, meaning the same as kike).[26] In Morocco in 1965, another Muslim writer noted that "the worst insult one Moroccan can make to another is to call him a Jew." Moroccans, as well as Idi Amin and a young, less-enlightened Anwar Sadat, received the sale of Hitler's massacre of the Jews "with delight" and awaited his return "to free the Arabs from Israel."[27]

Jewish existence under Islamic rule was never idyllic. While it is a pastime of some scholars to recite Jewish achievements in "the Golden Age of Spain," Gustave von Grunebaum points out, "It will be just as easy to cite a long inventory of persecutions, arbitrary confiscations, attempts at forcible conversion and pogroms."[28] George Sale, who made the first English translation of the Quran 120 years ago, stated that Muslims treat Jews as the most abject and contemptible creatures on earth. That attitude has been confirmed repeatedly by other observers. Eighty years ago, the scholar Armin Vambery, himself a convert to Islam, declared, "I do not know any more miserable, helpless, and pitiful individuals on God's earth than the Yahudi in those [Muslim] countries."[29] When the Turks took Yemen in 1872, the chief rabbi of Istanbul was asked what grievances Yemeni Jews had against their neighbors. The first complaint was molestation by schoolboys. When the Turkish government asked an assembly of notables to stop this nuisance, an old doctor of Muslim law stood up and explained that this stone throwing at Jews was an age-old custom. Shlomo Goitein agreed: "In former times and in remote places even today, it was common for Muslim schoolboys to stone Jews."[30] Princeton's Bernard Lewis concluded that "The golden age of equal rights was a myth, and belief in it was a result more than a cause of Jewish sympathy for Islam. The myth was invented in nineteenth-century Europe as a reproach to Christians—and taken up by Muslims in our time as a reproach to Jews."[31]

Since 1896, the development of modern, political Zionism has placed new tension on, and even destroyed, the traditional master–serf relationship that existed between Arab and Jew in the Middle East. An Arab world that could not tolerate the presence of a single, "arrogant" Jewish vizier in its history was now confronted by a modern state staffed with self-confident Jewish ministers. Unable to erase that shame, Arab anti-Semitism, the brew of thirteen centuries of intolerance, would now be channeled against captive Jewish populations, Sephardic Jews whom Maurice Roumani has called *asfal al-safilin,* the lowest of the low.

2

Arab-Jewish Relations in the Twentieth Century

Jews living in the Middle East in the twentieth century became the victims of a clash of cultures and nationalisms. Modern political Zionism, the product of 4,000 years of religious aspirations, the organizational genius of Theodor Herzl, and the reawakening of Jewish national consciousness, collided with a resurgence of Arab national pride. During World War I, Jews were issued a loosely phrased promise (the Balfour Declaration) that held out hope of restoring a Jewish state. Simultaneously, the Arabs believed that their role in campaigns of the Emir Faisal and T. E. Lawrence, including the liberation of Damascus, would signal an end to foreign domination. Instead, the Arabs found themselves shunted aside by the imperial powers, and demeaned under the rule of Mandates, which implied they were unfit to govern themselves.[1]

In order to appease Arabs in Palestine, the British designated Haj Amin el-Husseini as Grand Mufti of Jerusalem, a position that carried great prestige and wealth in 1921.[2] This Palestinian feudal lord proved instead to be a fiery demagogue capable of mobilizing Arab passions for the next thirty years. Responsible for riots in the Holy Land in 1921, 1929, and again in 1936–1939, Haj Amin continued his assault against the Western democracies from Beirut, Baghdad, and Tehran before ultimately taking up residence in Berlin in 1942. There he headed up the *Buro des Grossmufti,* which aided the Axis war effort through propaganda broadcasts to the Islamic world, teams of saboteurs, and Muslim troop levies from Yugoslavia. The Mufti sought and repeatedly won from Himmler, Hitler, and Ribbentrop statements of support for Arab nationalism. On several occasions, he visited concentration camps where he witnessed gassings of Jews.[3]

He suggested to Hitler that the Arab countries be granted the right "to solve the problem of the Jews living in Palestine or other Arab countries in a manner that conforms to the national and ethnic interests of the Arabs and to the solution of the Jewish question in the countries of Germany and Italy."[4] The Mufti wrote in his diary on November 9, 1944, "very rare diamond, the best saviour of the Arabs"—and under that, the name Eichmann.[5] When the war ended, Haj Amin was declared a war criminal by the United Nations. Despite a half-hearted search by the French in 1945, he managed to slip out of Europe and resume command of the Palestinian national movement for the next five years.

Had the career of the popular and charismatic Mufti been a singular instance of anti-Jewish activity on the part of a modern Arab leader, it would have been bad enough. The facts are otherwise. After 1935, Arab nationalists throughout the Middle East, deluding themselves that the fascists might grant independence, gravitated toward Germany and Italy in the superpowers' conflict. When Iraq declared a jihad against Britain in May 1941, Syria's Hashim Atasi, Lebanon's Riad as-Sulh, and Egypt's King Farouk all wired congratulatory telegrams to the Baghdad government. A year later, when Rommel's Afrika Korps was striking near El Alamein, Farouk, Egyptian war hero Aziz Ali al-Misri, and General Azzam Pasha were all placed under house arrest because Egypt's defense minister had defected to the Nazis. As troops in his Jordan Legion grumbled, Brigadier John Bagot Glubb Pasha lamented, "Every Arab force previously organized by us mutinied and refused to fight for us, or faded away in desertions."[6]

In his 1974 speech before the United Nations, Yasir Arafat evoked images of substantial Arab contributions to the Allied war effort.[7] The truth is somewhat different. During the war, the Allied high command declared North Africa out of bounds to Jews seeking temporary refuge, because of the fear of Muslim hostility. On the other hand, every conceivable able-bodied man, including Pole, Russian, and Czech, was welcomed to Palestine and Iran to help with the war effort—except Jews. Most Arab states (including Saudi Arabia, which had been subsidized with $50 million in Lend Lease) did not declare war against the Axis until the last week of February 1945, and then only because the Allies insisted that charter membership in the United Nations depended on such a declaration being issued before March 1.[8]

When World War II ended, evidence of Nazi atrocities against Jews in Europe could no longer be denied. The masses fled the displaced-persons camps and went to Palestine. Although Arab nationalists denied any culpability for the Holocaust, they turned against the survivors and their kinsmen. Quite soon a pattern of brutality emerged that consisted of the following.

Medieval Libels: Just as in Kielce, Poland, where survivors of the Holocaust were charged with ritual murder on July 4, 1946, Sephardic Jews were accused of trying to kidnap two Arab girls in San'a for ritual purposes in 1948, of giving poisoned sweets to an Arab child in Baghdad in May, 1947, and of dropping cholera microbes into the Euphrates near the Iraqi town of Ar-Ramādī in December, 1947.[9]

→*Pogroms:* Before and after the United Nations approved the partition of Palestine in November, 1947, most Jewish population centers in the Middle East were ravaged by anti-Semitic mobs. In Tripoli, Lebanon, fourteen Jews were killed in November 1945 and another forty-four in eastern Morocco in June, 1948. Vandals did $3 million's damage to Jewish institutions in Libya in 1945 and another $4.5 million in Aden in December, 1947. Ten people were killed and 350 were injured in Balfour Day protests in Cairo on November 2, 1945. During the summer and fall of 1948, fifty Jews died in Egypt, some in bomb blasts that rocked the pathetic hovels of the Cairo ghetto; others were mutilated in street attacks.[10]

→*Interference with Religious Rites:* Most Arab states banned the teaching of Hebrew. Rabbi Kurdagi of Beirut was forced to pay a £5 tax for each religious service. As early as November 18, 1945, the great synagogue in Aleppo was looted, its prayer books burned in the streets. By 1948, the great synagogue in Cairo had become the nonfunctioning tourist attraction it remains to this day. Twenty-five synagogues in Baghdad were closed and a year later, in August, 1949, the great Damascus synagogue was bombed, leaving twelve dead and twenty-six wounded.

→*Ouster from Jobs and Schools:* In Lebanon, where education was compulsory, Jews were dismissed from schools, save one missionary school where they were permitted to attend, provided they wore blue-and-white striped blouses. In Egypt, Jews were expelled from the bar, press, and banks. In Iraq, whose 1932 constitution guaranteed equality for all minorities, Jewish teachers were dismissed from public schools, and their own institutions received no state subsidies.[11]

→*Loss of Civil Rights:* Early on, Libya placed 3,000 Jews under protective custody to do forced labor. Virtually every Arab state emulated Iraq, which required Jews to carry a specially marked identity card and which passed a law on July 14, 1948 imposing the death penalty for the crime of Zionism. Sending a letter to Israel or attempting to flee the country might result in public execution of the kind that cost nine Jews their lives at Tahrir Square, Baghdad, on January 27, 1969.[12]

Boycott: Since its inception in 1945, the Arab League has maintained an economic boycott not only of Jewish institutions in Palestine/Israel, but also of foreign companies that trade with the Jewish state or, in some instances, that are identified with prominent Jewish personnel. States that subscribe to the boycott refuse postal, air, and road communications with Israel; will not sit on humanitarian international bodies, such as the United Nations Educational, Scientific, and Cultural Organization (UNESCO) and the Food and Agricultural Organization (FAO), with Israeli representatives; and implore the Federal Republic of Germany not to make reparations to Holocaust survivors who reside in Israel. As an extension of the Mufti's Central Boycott Office in Damascus dating back to the 1930s, the Arab League imposes stiff penalties (as much as ten years hard labor and fines in excess of $10,000) for violations.[13]

Confiscation: When Shafiq Ades of Basra, Iraq, was hanged in September,

1948, the state appropriated his assets valued at $20 million. Two years later, the government of Nuri es-Said took more than $120 million in frozen bank accounts and $300 million in property from Iraqi kinsmen. In 1956, Egypt expelled 20,000 Jews, giving each seven days' notice and the opportunity to take with them a suit of clothes and some pocket money. In August, 1971, the Association of Jewish Victims of Egyptian Persecution claimed it was seeking reparations in the amount of approximately $1 billion ($300 million in property, $200 million confiscated religious articles, $400 million personal compensation). All told, the figure for confiscation may surpass $2 billion.[14]

Historically, Jews have been denigrated as inferiors and especially harassed since the creation of the state of Israel. Jews fled lands, where they had resided for centuries before the Arab conquest, and went to Israel. Seventy thousand came from Yemen in 1949–1950, in what romantically, if inaccurately, has been labeled Operation Magic Carpet and 130,000 arrived from Iraq in 1950–1951 under Operation Ali Baba. During those early years, 75,000 came from Egypt, 40,000 from Libya, 30,000 from Syria, 9,000 from Aden, and 10,000 from Lebanon. These refugees were joined by another 40,000 from Iran and 37,000 from Turkey. Before the North African colonies of France and Italy achieved independence in 1956–1962, another 160,000 Jews, who realized, as few Western pundits did, that their presence was undesired, fled Morocco, Tunisia, and Algeria. In the past twenty-five years, another 180,000 have emigrated. According to Yehuda Dominitz, recently retired as director general of the *Aliyah* and Absorption Department of the Jewish Agency in Jerusalem, nearly $300 million (at $535 per person) was spent on initial absorption of these refugees, $3 billion on housing, $400 million for developing *moshavim*, $300 million for public-works projects that trained immigrants, and $2.5 billion for other forms of economic development. Combined with health and education projects, Israel has spent approximately $11 billion of its own money,[15] not a cent coming from the United Nations or its subsidiary Relief and Works Agency (UNRWA), which has underwritten care of Palestinian refugees for the past forty years.

THE STATUS OF JEWS TODAY

At one time, approximately 1,000,000 Sephardic Jews were scattered among the Islamic countries. Today the figure is less than 70,000 (see table 1).[16] Those who remain in ancestral lands live a precarious existence, subsidized in part by the Joint Distribution Committee (JDC) (an American relief agency that has spent more than $150 million on Jews in the Muslim world since 1914, a sum exceeded only by assistance to Israel itself), Alliance Israelite (the French-based humanitarian organization that specializes in education), ORT (Organization for Rehabilitation through Training, an international women's group that offers job training), and OSE (a Jewish health agency organized in Russia in 1912). Wherever they are, Jews insist their lives are better under the current regime. A nation-by-nation summary reveals, however, that discrimination persists and that what

Table 1
Jews in the Islamic World, 1987

Nation	Pre-1948	Current	Arrived	Outside Contacts
Afghanistan	5,000	60	300 B.C.	Passover supplies
Algeria	130-140,000	300	200 B.C.	Aged care welfare through French Consul
Bahrein	400	10	1000 B.C.	No information
Egypt	75,000	250	600 B.C.	Passover, welfare, aged Memorial libraries
Iran	90-100,000	28,000	600 B.C.	No contacts permitted
Iraq	125,000	400	600 B.C.	Limited mail
Lebanon	5,000	300	1000 B.C.	Able to meet own needs
Libya	38,000	7-20	500 B.C.	No contacts permitted
Morocco	265-300,000	10,000	200 B.C.	Education, aged care, summer camp, food, health
Sudan	400	50	400 B.C.	No information
Syria	40,000	4,500	1000 B.C.	Education, relief
Tunisia	105,000	3,000	200 B.C.	Aged, food, housing, education
Turkey	80,000	24,000	1000 B.C.	"Nervous" about outside contacts
Yemen (North and South)	55,000	1,000	1000 B.C.	Inadequate information

Note: The Muslim Conquest of the Middle East and North Africa occurred between 630 and 750 A.D.

Sources: American Jewish Committee and Joint Distribution Committee

passes for stability in the Middle East might suddenly deteriorate into a life-threatening condition.

Morocco

Morocco is the Arab state with the largest number of Jews (10,000). Nearly half the current JDC budget for Middle Eastern Jews, $2.2 million, goes to programs for visiting nurses, surgical and medical care for the aged, maternity and infant care, job training, cemetery maintenance, school lunches, and surplus commodities. King Hassan, a modern, moderate ruler, has outwitted several coup attempts. His popularity was bolstered when he championed Morocco's claim to 100,000 miles of the western Sahara and his international reputation was enhanced by support of the Camp David peace agreement. Moroccan Jews cannot be faulted if they wonder what will happen if these policies prove to be failures. Morocco is an emerging nation, where only 24 percent of the people are literate, the per capita income is $670 per year, and the doctor:patient ratio is 1:11,143.[17] It was not very long ago that Moroccan Jews were encouraged to flee by supporters of the Palestine Liberation Organization (PLO) who posted walls with warnings to "Jewish worshippers of the dollar, weapon-mongers, organizers of Sabotage, Mafia gangs, and servants of Satan" that they would "enter your homes, smash the skulls of your old people, put out the eyes of your children, behead your parents, slash the bellies of your wives."[18] According to Dr. George Gruen of the American Jewish Committee (AJC), the governing phrase for Morocco is *pas de problème* (no problem). However, one Jew told Gruen confidentially, *"Pas de problème sauf tous les problèmes."*[19]

Tunisia

Tunisia numbers only 3,000 Jews, down from a time when more than 100,000 lived in the fabled Semitic land of Carthage. This was the first French colony in North Africa to obtain independence and its President Habib Bourguiba was regarded as a thoughtful, fair man. Recently, however, the eighty-seven-year-old Bourguiba was deposed. There are no comparable leaders within his Neo-Destour party, which some feel has been in power too long. Tunisia's peasant population is not much better off than that of Morocco (literacy 32 percent, per capital income $950), is disturbed by the rising cost of bread (115 percent in 1984 alone), and is receptive to fundamentalist and pan-Arab causes. When the PLO was temporarily forced to evacuate Beirut in 1983, Tunisia permitted the organization to establish headquarters in Tunis. The result has been to nudge Tunisia (bombed by Israel in October, 1985 and the scene of an attack by a berserk policeman against Jews in the Djerba synagogue at Simchat Torah the same year) toward a confrontation stance vis-à-vis Israel.[20]

Yemen

There are not supposed to be any Jews in Yemen. Israeli scholar S. D. Goitein once declared that all the Jews had gone in 1950.[21] Yemenis themselves are surprised to learn that nearly 1,000 Jews remain in remote districts of Suq 'Anan and Amran 50–100 miles north of San'a, the capital. According to one young businessman who returned from the district in February 1988, some of the Jews may never have heard of Operation Magic Carpet and thus were left behind. For the moment, they function without official harassment from the government of President Ali Abdallah. The Jews trade in jewelry and maintain a few schools. They receive Bibles and tefillin from Satmarers in the United States (a Chasidic sect that opposes the existence of Israel on messianic grounds). Disputes between Muslims and Jews are settled by an Arab tribal shaykh. If the people feel menaced, they may appeal to the government or the U.S. Embassy. Generally, however, the Jews of Yemen are apolitical. Zionism is condemned in the country's national charter, and in 1983 two Westerners were arrested as Zionist spies. It is possible to send mail to Israel via a third party. Emigration is not permitted, although the government did recently agree to allow twenty-five relatives to renew family acquaintances.[22] Yemen's problems are all too common to the region. Fewer than 1 in 12 of its 5,000,000 people are literate and the per capita income is $580. Infant mortality is approximately 200–250 and life expectancy is 40–42 years. Its neighbor to the south, the Yemen Democratic Republic, is radical Marxist. The two nations have waged border wars periodically since 1971. To complicate matters, oil has been discovered, 200 million barrels of known reserves, in this ancient land. What it means for Jews who still wear the *zunnar* and pay the *jizyah* is difficult to tell.

Lebanon

For at least eighteen years, the few Jews (300?) remaining in Lebanon have lived in terror of kidnap and murder. Even before the onset of the civil war in 1974, which left this multinational state dysfunctional, Jews had been terrorized by the disappearance of their community secretary, Albert Elia. On the morning of September 6, 1971, the sixty-seven-year-old Elia was taken as he left his home, bound for the community building. First reports suggested he may have been kidnapped by Palestinians. Later, two Beirut newspapers (*L'Orient le Jour* and *An-Nahar*) reported that Elia was removed to Syrian territory at the instruction of "one of the organizations of the Arab states."[23] Elia's whereabouts remain a mystery. But since his disappearance, Lebanese Jews have tried, with limited success, to avoid provoking anti-Zionist gangs. A Beirut synagogue was attacked when Israel invaded Lebanon in 1982. A wave of abductions began in 1984 when sixty-eight-year-old Isaac Sasson, director of a pharmaceutical company and head of the community, disappeared. Within the year, five more prominent Jews were kidnapped. In the winter of 1985–1986, four Lebanese Jews (a department store accountant with three children, a seventy-year-old mathematics professor, a pediatrician who doubled as vice president of the Jewish community, and a fourth man simply described as a Mossad agent) were murdered by a Shiite splinter group calling itself the Organization of the World's Oppressed—all the bodies bore marks of torture. The body of Dr. Elie Hallak, known as the Doctor of the Poor because he treated patients without distinction to background, was never returned to his family, although Hezbollah (a terrorist organization) announced his execution on February 19, 1986.[24] Nabi Berri, the AMAL (Afwaj al-Muqawauma al-Lubnaniya, Battalions of the Lebanese Resistance) leader who has become so familiar to Americans, decries a policy that "only helps Zionism and has nothing to do with patriotism or the struggle." Another observer warns, "No one is safe in Lebanon these days, not least of all the Jews. . . . The death knell for Lebanese Jewry has been sounded."[25]

Egypt

More than 30 years have passed since Gamal Nasser expelled the bulk of Egypt's Jews. It now is possible for an American Jew to stroll through Cairo's alleys and bazaars or peek in at classes of the al-Azhar University without feeling great tension. Egyptian guides eagerly point out reconstruction efforts at the oldest synagogue in Cairo, which dates back nearly 1,500 years. (Tourists who have been here more than once note there has been no progress on restoring the *genizah* or synagogue.)[26] The government welcomes foreign assistance for its 250 Jews, including thirty rabbis and many elderly. The JDC helps with food and wine for Passover as well as financial assistance for the Jewish Memorial Library, which is cataloging 60,000 volumes found in seventeen Cairo synagogues.[27] Downtown Cairo is aglitter at night with restaurants, hotels, and automobiles on boulevards crossing the Nile. Graceful stucco apartments are being constructed along the Mediterranean near Al-'Arīsh in the Sinai. But Egypt, too, has problems. A nation of forty-eight million people, its population doubles every twenty-five years. Its housing minister estimates that 80 percent of all housing in Egypt will be substandard by the year 2000, despite new oil revenues. Anyone who has been to Luxor and seen how appreciative hansom drivers are for a £1 tip (40¢) will understand that they are desperately poor (per capita income $400–800 per year). And although Egypt under Hosni Mubarak has extended the relatively enlightened programs initiated by Anwar Sadat, anti-Jewish cartoons appear in newspapers, Egypt recognizes the legitimacy of the Palestine Liberation Organization (PLO) declaration of independence, and sounds emanating from its mosques are those of the blind mullah Keshk, exhorting the faithful to revert to seventh-century practices of Islam.

Iraq

Although no foreign relief contacts are permitted for the 400 Jews who survive in Iraq, conditions have improved since spring 1973, when eighteen were jailed without cause and several others murdered in their homes.[28] When columnist Nick Thimmesch visited Baghdad in 1983, he discovered an aging community that was able to maintain its one functioning synagogue and to do business. Rabbi Rouben Naji Alias said, "Everything is better now. There were bad feelings toward Jews before [Saddam] Hussein took over the Baath Party. Hussein is good for us. I met Hussein several times and I like him."[29]

Hussein is supposedly committed to a socialist, secular state, therefore, Jews may correspond with relatives abroad (the mail is censored), emigrate, and enlist to fight in Iraq's ceaseless struggle with Iran. Because conditions improved under Hussein, one Jewish family that had left the country decided to return. Dr. Heskel Hadad, a New York physician who fled Iraq in 1950 and now heads the American Committee to Rescue Iraqi Jews, reported, "The Jew is always there and could become the scapegoat any time Iraq needs one again."[30]

Iran

Iran is not an Arab nation, but its remaining 28,000 Jews have been swept up in the vortex of Islamic fundamentalism. A decade ago, it would have been deemed absurd to suggest there could ever be a problem for the Jews of Iran. They were prosperous, well integrated in the economic, political, and social fabric of the most Westernized state in the Gulf region. In discussions with Iranian-Jewish students about the Holocaust, they consistently asked questions such as "Why didn't the German Jews get out before Hitler? Didn't they realize what was going to happen?'' Since its own nightmare descended on Iran in 1979, perhaps another 30,000 Jews have fled, including teachers, doctors, journalists, engineers, and some of the very students who asked questions about Germany. Those who remain, as elsewhere in the Islamic world, are the poor, the aged, the wishful thinkers with or without property, and the ones who are always trapped. The *Anjoman Kalimian,* the central Jewish body, still meets and offers petitions to the Imam Ruhollah Khomeini. Synagogues are still open. But with the introduction of Quranic studies and the infusion of anti-Semitic polemics in public schools, most parents send their children to Jewish institutions. The terror of revolutionary tribunals and comites has been subdued in recent years (the maximum number of Jews under detention at the present time is estimated at twenty-five). The persecution of Jews has not been as extensive as that instituted against Baha'is. Yet Iran's Jews know that Zionism is now a capital offense. They recall that Iran's leading mall builder (Habib Elghanian), two members of a family that owned a chain of hotels, a sixty-seven-year-old translator, and a fifty-one-year-old businessman from Hamadan were executed between 1979 and 1983 on trumped-up charges of spying for Israel, treason, drug dealing, and/or ''corruption on earth.'' The Beroukhim family was charged with permitting their hotels to be spy centers for Americans and Israelis and offering in their gift shops Israeli coins. The translator, Simon Farzami, was convicted of giving foreign intelligence information about PLO members. The evidence allegedly came from shredded documents taken from the U.S. embassy and restored ''with much difficulty and great care.'' Businessman Albert Danielpour was shot to death on June 4, 1980, after being condemned by the Ayatollah Khalkhali for the crimes of ''suppressing the Palestinian revolution, spying for the CIA and Israel, and importing honey from Israel. Mr. Danielpour left a widow and 3 young children.''[31] The Khomeini regime has guaranteed no harm to the Jewish community as a whole, provided it behaves, and there is probably a connection between Israeli arms shipments to this hostile nation and the hostage status of Iran's Jews. As one source has put it, ''Jews are not presently being singled out for extra measures. The situation is not life-threatening, but Iran is an uncomfortable and unpromising place to live.''[32]

Turkey

For years, Dr. Gruen has described Turkey as ''schizophrenic.''[33] On the one hand, there is a tradition of toleration that dates back to the time when the Bayezid II of the Ottoman Empire welcomed the expelled Jews from Spain to his realm. Jews worked closely with the Young Turks, the Committee of Union and Progress, which brought down the Ottoman despotism in 1909. Since the end of World War I and the revolution of Kemal Ataturk, Turkey has distanced itself from Arabs and fundamentalism. With the exception of the Shah's Iran, it was the only Muslim state to maintain normal diplomatic relations with Israel. In recent years, however, there has been a cooling of these relations. When the

Begin government formally united Jerusalem as the eternal capital of Israel, the Turkish Consulate in Jerusalem was closed and a second secretary assigned to the post. Turkish air flights to Israel were halted. Israel, which had participated in an annual fair at Izmir for thirty years, was barred on technical grounds that its application was received too late. Some Israeli scholars were "disinvited" to conferences at the last moment. The presence of Khomeini at its borders, the activities of Armenian terrorists, additional dependence on foreign oil subsidies, and the growth of the National Salvation party (an Islamic fundamentalist group) and the right-wing National Action party have altered the outlook for Turkey. For example, (1) in 1980, Islamic extremists staged the first of several violent anti-Zionist demonstrations in Konya, (2) in the summer of 1982, the Turkish government let it be known that if prominent Jewish scholars participated in an international conference on genocide to be held in Tel Aviv, Turkey would not guarantee passage across its borders for Jews fleeing Syria or Iran, nor could it guarantee the safety of its own Jewish population from "spontaneous" demonstrations, (3) 150,000 Turks working in Arab lands annually send home $1.3 billion, more than all the Turks living and working in Europe, and (4) the PLO has grown in support and cooperates with anti-Semitic, right-wing organizations in Turkey. The best that can be said of the 20,000 Jews who live in Turkey (18,000 in Istanbul alone) is that they are nervous. Jews are free to emigrate and take their goods with them. Most have relatives in Israel. One official Jewish school operates with 300 students. They are not free, however, to maintain national organizations. Each community is supposed to take care of its own needs. Nor are they permitted to maintain international contacts. In Turkey, every B'nai B'rith lodge functions as an autonomous unit. Turkey likes to think of itself as different from other Middle Eastern countries, but three military coups in the past twenty years seems to indicate a closer kinship to Iraq than Great Britain. Official government reaction to the September 6, 1986 Istanbul massacre, where nineteen Jews were machine-gunned in a synagogue on Rosh Hashanah, also suggests otherwise. The Evren junta issued a stern denunciation of the PLO atrocity, yet made no effort to suppress Palestinian propaganda in the country. And when the victims were buried, not a single Muslim leader or high-ranking government official joined the Christians and Jews who participated in the funeral.[34]

SUMMARY

Long before I encountered the Imam of Columbus, I returned from Toronto wearing a button that had been given to me by a member of the Canadian Committee for Rescue of Jews in Arab Lands. It was at a time when most American Jews were just beginning to protest the treatment of Jews in Russia. A colleague walked by and, observing the six-sided star on the button, commented, "Oh, a Save Soviet Jewry button." Then, noting its inscription calling for the rescue of Jews from Arab lands, he offered sympathetically, "Why don't you just come up with a button that says, 'Save the Jews!' "

A bit harsh, perhaps, but cogent for the 20 Jews who remain in Libya, the 50 in Sudan, the 300 in Algeria, and the 60 in Afghanistan. Throughout the Middle East, Jewish institutions are under assault. The thousand-year-old cemetery of Salaam Shabazzi in Yemen has been razed, cemeteries in Egypt, Libya, and Algeria laid waste for road projects. The El-Kebira synagogue in Tripoli and six others in Cairo have been converted to mosques. Pogroms persist, and when the culprits are apprehended (as in the case of twelve youths responsible for looting a synagogue in Algiers in January, 1977), they are given suspended sentences.[35]

The best that can be said for any minority—Maronite, Kurd, Copt, Baha'i, Zoroastrian, or Jew—living in the Middle East today is that its status is tenuous. The history of the region confirms that whenever *dhimmi* feel secure and comfortable, they may be attacked. Animosity toward Jews appears to be especially deep rooted. Despite public affirmations from governments of Semitic brotherhood (offered for consumption by the Western press, the Vatican, or international forums), Jews remain the first and likeliest victims of Arab frustration and rage. Arab anti-Semitism is the product of religious rivalry, fundamentalist distortion, shame at Israel's existence, and anti-Western fury. The Islamic Middle East remains a prison for most Jews, or if you prefer, a cage. That was precisely the description used by several sources who offered information about the last and most severely oppressed group—the Jews of Syria.

3

A Humanitarian Gesture

On December 30, 1983, Jesse Jackson, the civil rights leader who was making his first bid for the presidency of the United States, arrived in Damascus, Syria, on what President Ronald Reagan called "a mission of mercy."[1] Accompanying Jackson were Reverend William Howard, past president of the National Council of Churches; Dr. Thelma Adair, national president of Church Women United; Louis Farrakhan, leader of a sect of Black Muslims; Reverend Wyatt T. Walker; and Jack Mendelsohn of the Unitarian-Universalist Association.[2] The object of this delegation was to obtain the release of an American airman, downed in fighting in Lebanon.

Naval Lieutenant Robert Goodman was serving as bombardier–navigator in an A6E Intruder when it was hit by Syrian surface-to-air missiles over central Lebanon on December 4. Goodman parachuted and was quickly taken into custody by Syrian troops. His copilot Lieutenant Mark A. Lange was not as fortunate. Shortly after crash landing the plane, Lange, who was riddled with wounds and who may have lost a leg, died.[3] True to the hostage syndrome, Lieutenant Goodman, who was permitted to meet privately with a representative of the International Red Cross, commented that his treatment by the Syrians was "pretty good."[4] What he did not know was that while he was in custody, dozens of columns were being written about him in journals of the free world and that more than 60,000 pieces of mail, many of them Christmas cards, had been sent to boost his spirits.

One special communication was not in the form of holiday tidings. Almost immediately, Jackson acted to assist the black airman. In a cable to Syria's President Hafaz al-Assad, Jackson evoked images of Goodman's wife and two daughters (aged seven and two and one-half) and appealed for the airman's release "as a humanitarian gesture."[5] Responding to this request, the Syrian government, which earlier had puffed that Goodman would not be exchanged until "the war is over,"[6] invited Jackson to discuss a number of issues related to the Middle East conflict. Four years earlier, in 1979, Jackson had met with Assad, Yasir Arafat, and King Hussein while on an informational tour with black American leaders and was regarded with some esteem in the region.

While some legal savants pondered whether Jackson violated the Logan Act (a law dating to 1799 that prohibits individuals from negotiating on behalf of the United States), the *New York Times* criticized his "self-serving" ploy that was "undercutting authority."[7] Jackson's fourteen-man contingent arrived in Damascus, where it was met by Deputy Foreign Minister Isam Annayeb and U.S. Ambassador Robert Paganelli. Three preliminary meetings with government officials were arranged, followed by a twenty-minute session with President Assad and an interview with Lieutenant Goodman. Two days later (January 3, 1984) Jackson was asked to extend his visit. Then, the Syrians announced that they were releasing Goodman to the custody of Reverend Jackson. Whereas U.S. officials pointed out the release was "unconditional," the Syrians expressed hope that the action might lead to the end of U.S. military involvement in Lebanon, "which has contributed pain and suffering to Lebanon, to the area, and to the American people." Their official communiqué on the matter indicated that Goodman's release came in answer to "the human appeal of the Rev. Jesse Jackson to President Hafez al-Assad."[8]

When Lieutenant Goodman stepped out of the airplane at Andrews Air Force Base a day later to the embrace of his loved ones, it was impossible not to be moved. For the remainder of the month, Lieutenant Goodman's story was played out in every dimension (the reaction of his mother, wife, and children) on the television networks. Newspapers in the hinterlands faithfully reprinted wire-service stories from the more-knowing *New York Times* or *Washington Post*. In consecutive issues, *Newsweek* hailed Jackson's "appointment in Damascus" as a victory in "a Syria Primary."[9] *U.S. News and World Report* and *Time* magazines echoed these reports.[10] In his moment of glory, Jackson was magnanimous, lauding President Reagan, the State Department, and Ambassador Paganelli. There was also praise for Syria and its president who had "used this opportunity to seize an initiative . . . to save this generation from disaster." Jackson said "I would hope that the cycle of pain is now broken and that this mission of peace will take us to an everlasting peace."[11]

All of that euphoria came at a time before Western intelligence sources could provide evidence linking Assad's government to the bombing of the U.S. Embassy in Beirut in 1983, in which 17 Americans were killed; to the October, 1983 bombing of the U.S. Marine Corps barracks in Lebanon, in which 241 Americans died; to the suicide bombing of the U.S. Embassy annex in Beirut in 1984; to the midsummer 1985 hijacking of a TWA airliner, in which American Seal Robert Stethem was bludgeoned and murdered; to the grenade and machine-gun attacks at principal airports in Rome and Vienna in December, 1985, in which 19 people were killed and 114 wounded; to the bombing of the German-Arab Friendship Society building in West Berlin in March, 1986, which left 9 people severely wounded; or to the attempt to sabotage an El Al aircraft bound from London to Tel Aviv with more than 300 people aboard in April, 1986.[12]

Goodman's release came at a time when Western journalists regarded Muammar al-Qaddafi as the bogeyman of international terrorism, not Assad, the likable moderate who in 1970 stabilized a country that had been vibrated by forty coups since 1946. Not Assad, the dapper, smiling statesman, himself a member of a minority sect, who was responsible for the bloody purge of more than 30,000 Sunnites in Hama in February, 1982 and whose troops in the Bekaa Valley provided training and sanctuary for kidnappers of Islamic jihad. Not Assad, whose diplomats may have given money and passports to Abu Nidal's killers aboard the *Achille Lauro*, and who were probably responsible for the assassination of Bashir Gemayel, the one Lebanese who may have ended the civil war in that land.

It also occurred shortly before Jackson squandered much goodwill, which his coup with Lieutenant Goodman had won him, by employing the racist epithets *Hymies* and *Hymietown* to refer to Jews and New York City. That gaffe, uttered at a Washington airport cafeteria on January 25, 1984, was only compounded days later when in an address, Jackson suggested that Jews in the Holocaust had marched silently to their deaths in Nazi gas chambers.[13] As Jackson lashed out at what he deemed a conspiracy against his candidacy,[14] and colleague Louis Farrakhan warned the press and especially black reporter Milton Coleman of dire consequences,[15] other Democratic presidential hopefuls, led by Walter Mondale, mildly rebuked Jackson for his lamentable choice of words.[16]

There was another story from Syria breaking at precisely the time of Lieutenant Goodman's release that should have commanded the attention of the free world, but did not. None of the network news broadcasts, the weekly journals, or the *New York Times*, which printed more than fifty articles on Lieutenant Goodman, reported this event. A brutal murder took place in Aleppo, on December 28, 1983, just as Jesse Jackson was about to depart for Syria. The victims were three Jews—Lillian Antebi Abadi, aged twenty-four, and her infant children Josef, six, and Sandy, three. Mrs. Abadi was in her fourth month of pregnancy when she and her children were shot to death in their apartment.

To this day, there is some confusion over what exactly happened to the Abadi family. From what can be pieced together, it appears that Mr. Abadi (who now resides in the United States), like many other Syrian Jews, was an artisan working in gold. For several months, Assad's government had been having trouble with Muslim fundamentalists in both Hama and Aleppo. Security police conducted sweeps through a number of districts, including those where Jews lived (though why Jews would be giving assistance to Sunnite fanatics was never explained). During one of these searches, two or more of Rifaat al-Assad's militia observed a quantity of gold in Abadi's house. Some sources suggest that Abadi secretly may have been negotiating his family's release from Syria with these members of the militia or the *Muhabarat* (state secret police). In 1982, Lillian and her husband had been permitted to visit family in the United States. As a condition against their return, their three-year-old daughter was detained with relatives in Aleppo. On the day of the murders, the theory runs, several disgruntled members of the militia went to the house either to extort more money from Abadi or to rob the family. Finding him not at home, they simply massacred everyone they found. What made the killings more grotesque was that all three of the victims were disemboweled.[17]

According to the official Syrian version of the tale, the three men who killed the Abadis (and a minister) were punished. Responding angrily to an international conference on the status of Jews in Syria held in Paris in October 1984, Syrian Ambassador Youssef Chakkour declared, "In fact, the government has deemed it necessary, as a deterrent, in Aleppo to execute three criminals whose victims were an Armenian pastor and the wife of Jewish jeweler who had three children. The need to safeguard the welfare of confessional minorities, Jews and others, is obvious."[18] Apparently, the government of Israel accepts this story, for a spokesman repeated it to me, with minor variations.[19]

Others disagree. According to a rabbi who fled Aleppo, "No one ever was arrested for those murders. Now tell me, do you think Assad or the Syrian government would have waited three years if the victims were not Jews?"[20] Says another source, a prominent businessman, "There was no arrest. We were told the government looked around. Don't you believe it for a minute that there was a determined search for the murderers. You don't hang an Arab for killing a Jew in Syria."[21] A third source, an Israeli whose profession is relief and rescue work with Jews from Arab countries, told me, "Even if we see that it may have been a personal problem, between her husband and a few soldiers, that's an example of how Syrian Jews live. They are not protected. Even in a minimum of problems between the husband and the army, they can kill his children. Till today nobody's been arrested or punished."[22]

In March, 1984, when the horror of the Abadi killings was still fresh, 300 Jewish activists rallied at the Ontario legislature in Toronto's Queen's Park at a memorial service for the family. They listened as Rabbi Gunther Plaut, himself a refugee from Nazism, said, "Lillian Abadi was guilty of nothing but her descent." Speaking for her, Plaut added, "Do something for my people who are still alive. Mourn not for me alone, but mourn for the loss of freedom."[23]

There are obvious differences between the cases of Lillian Abadi and Lieutenant Goodman that may help account for the discrepancy of concern and press coverage. Americans naturally would be interested in the fate of one of their airmen who was downed while on an official mission in what has proved to be hostile territory. In statement after statement issued through December, 1983, Secretary of State George Schultz, Under Secretary Lawrence Eagleburger, and

Deputy Secretary Kenneth Dam echoed President Reagan's remarks: "Yes, we want that young man back. We're going to make every effort to get him back as quickly as possible."[24] Mrs. Abadi, on the other hand, was like the victims of riots in Sri Lanka or South Africa, faceless foreigners, innocents, to be sure, but not our responsibility. Her story, typical of so many in Syria, smacked of propaganda and Americans had had their fill of Jewish atrocity tales.

One who was very concerned over what image this case might project for Syria was Hafaz al-Assad. When his military junta seized absolute control of the government by ousting Ba'athist crony Salah Jedid in the fall of 1970, Assad inherited Syria's Jewish problem as well. This was a community rooted in antiquity (several synagogues in the Aleppo district supposedly were built by David's general Joab or the prophets Elijah and Elisha). Repeatedly throughout history, Jews in peril had returned to this ancient land, from Babylon after the sixth-century captivity and from Spain and Portugal in the time of the Inquisition and Expulsion in the fifteenth century. After World War I, the Jewish population in Syria grew to more than 60,000 as many Sephardic Jews, attracted by the fairly enlightened policies of the French Mandatory, arrived from Turkey. Jews prospered in business, agriculture, and the professions, and they began to feel comfortable and secure in their adopted homes. In Damascus, there were ten synagogues, a number of Torah academies, and Alliance Israelite schools where multilingual studies were encouraged. Much of Syria's foreign trade and tourism, as in neighboring Iraq, was in the hands of Jews. The prominent daily, *L'Orient*, was founded by an Egyptian Jews. Nearly all of the professorships at the prestigious University of Damascus were held by European Jews.[25]

Generally, Jews were still regarded with disdain as *dhimmi*. They endured episodes of persecution: in 1840 when the Damascus ghetto was ravaged in the wake of a ritual murder libel and again in the 1860s and 1920s when Druze warriors attacked anyone they regarded as outsiders. According to one Israeli source, "The year 1929 was a turning-point in the lives of the Jews of Syria."[26] At precisely the time when Jews, conscious of riots taking place in Jerusalem and Hebron, were responding to Zionism, Syria's mullahs were delivering incendiary speeches in the mosques. In the years that followed, ultra-nationalist groups such as the Syrian National party of Antun Saadah, the National Bloc, an-Nadi al-Arabi, the Council for the Defense of Arab Palestine, the Istiqlal Club, and the Iron Shirts made common cause with fascists against Britain and France.

From 1936 through 1945, Syria's Jews served as convenient scapegoats for the nationalists. When the British suppressed the Grand Mufti's Arab Higher Committee, elements of this Palestinian clique, which had close dealings with Nazi figures Adolf Eichmann and Baldur von Shirach, transferred their activities to Damascus. What followed was a series of attacks on Jews and their institutions, knifings in the streets, kidnappings, and arson. When France capitulated to Germany in 1940, its provincials reflected the new order, offering up radio broadcasts to the Middle East that suggested that Winston Churchill and Franklin Roosevelt intended to incorporate all of Syria, as well as Palestine, into a new Zionist state.[27]

When World War II ended, the profascist sympathies of the Syrians were conveniently forgotten and the state was admitted into the United Nations. While its ministers fulminated against a partition of Palestine, Syria stepped up domestic pressure against its own Jews. Anti-Zionist riots took place as early as March 20, 1945. In June of that year, Jacques Franco, assistant headmaster of the Aliance school in Damascus, was murdered "in broad daylight."[28] Although the governments of Shukry al-Kuwatli (1945–1949 and 1955–1958), Husni al-Zaim (March–August 1949), and Hashim Atasi (1949–1951) proclaimed equal protection for all Syrian citizens, the status of Jews deteriorated. As David Sitton, president of the Sephardic Community of Jerusalem, wrote, "With the creation of the State of Israel, the Syrian Jewish community was doomed to extinction."[29] At that time, there were more demonstrations, beatings, and rapes. Dozens of houses of worship were attacked, such as the August, 1949 bombing of the main Damascus synagogue noted previously. The government launched a vicious anti-Semitic campaign in the press, promoted the international Arab boycott of Jewish businesses or friends of Jews, froze millions of dollars in bank accounts, confiscated the property of Jews who fled the country, and threatened to impose the death penalty on anyone helping displaced persons fleeing Europe to reach Israel.[30]

According to a report submitted to the United Nations Economic and Social Council by the World Jewish Congress in February, 1948, "The number of unemployed Jews grows from day to day . . . the economic life of the Jews is almost completely paralyzed."[31] And yet, when representatives of Syria's Jewish community were given the opportunity to testify before the Anglo-American Committee of Inquiry on Palestine, which visited Damascus in March, 1946, they behaved in a manner all too typical of Syria's leadership in the postwar period. Given twenty minutes to comment on their status, the Jewish spokesman offered a one-sentence account that told how his people were happy, suffering no discrimination, that their situation was excellent and they wanted nothing to do with Zionism. According to Bartley C. Crum, a committee member, the statement took "forty-five seconds of his allotted time." When Judge Joseph Hutcheson, heading the subcommittee, pressed the spokesman whether he had anything else to say, the Syrian Jew shook his head. As the Jewish delegation departed, Muslim spectators who sat by bemused suposedly murmured, "They knew what was best for them."[32]

Years later, the discrepancy between official statements prepared for public consumption and the reality of persecution remains. Although the 156 articles of Syria's revolutionary consitution proclaim "freedom is a sacred right," "the state shall guarantee the personal freedom of citizens and safeguard their dignity and freedom," "every citizen shall have the right to participate in the political, economic, social and cultural life of the country," and "no one shall be subjected to physical or moral torture, or to treatment outrageous to dignity,"[33] such grandiloquent phrases apparently did not apply to the 5,000 Jews remaining in Syria when Assad took power in 1970. In an age when most attention was focused on the plight of Soviet Jewry, Abba Eban informed the Israeli Knesset, "The situation of Syrian Jewry is indeed the gravest."[34] It was an assessment shared by a number of experts. Dr. Heskel Haddad, president of the American Committee for Rescue and Resettlement of Iraqi Jews, wrote, "The Jews of Syria, Egypt, Iraq have virtually become beggars and paupers."[35] General Lucius Clay, president of the Committee of Concern for Minorities in Arab Lands; Alain Poher, president of the French Senate and the International Committee for Jews in Arab Countries; Sadrudin Agha Khan, U.N. High Commissioner for Refugees; and Israeli Ambassador Joel Barromi all condemned Syrian policies in 1971–1972.

There was a familiar ring to Syria's program of discrimination. Jews endured religious harassment. Licenses for services had to be purchased from the state police (*Muhabarat*), which monitored their length and content. Prayer books were censored, to eliminate references to the ancient kingdom of Israel or its religious counterpart. In Al-Qāmishlī, there were public burnings of phylacteries and other religious articles. Synagogues in Aleppo and Damascus were stoned repeatedly.

Arab headmasters were put in charge of Jewish schools, which, as in Iraq, received no state subsidies. The teaching of Hebrew or Jewish history in Jewish schools was prohibited. Public instruction reflected the statement of Minister of Education Suleyman al-Khash who said in May, 1968, "Hatred is sacred." Third-year textbooks in the schools taught that Israel lay "at the heart of the Arab nation." Extermination was a necessary preliminary to the renaissance of the Arab people. Israel "ought to be strangled, its Zionist bandits thrown into the sea."[36] Another text, composed by university professors, taught that Jews had been dispersed throughout the world because it was their nature to be vicious and rapacious, "the enemies of mankind."[37] Small wonder that the few Jews who were admitted to the university level were barred from studying "sensitive" subjects such as electronics or engineering.

Jews were required to live in ghettos and not permitted to travel more than 3 or 4 kilometers from their homes. (By contrast 500,000 Muslims visited Lebanon in 1971 alone.) Anyone attempting to flee the country could be jailed and tortured for three months or more. Jews were required to carry identity cards with the word *Mussawi* (follower of Moses) broadly scrawled in red ink. In Al-Qāmishlī, Jewish homes and stores were required to bear a red sign (the color connoting uncleanliness). Under a law dated February 8, 1967, all government employees and members of the Syrian armed forces were barred from trading with any Jewish establishment in Syria. A list of boycotted businesses was supplied by the government.[38] In some instances, Jews were barred from making food purchases themselves and had to rely on Syrian friends to keep them from starving. Jews could not own or drive automobiles or have telephones.

Jews could not serve in the Syrian armed forces, but had to pay $600 to secure exemption certificates. Jews could not sell property. In the event of death or illegal emigration, property was transferred to the state, which disposed of it either through sale or grant to Palestinians. Members of Saiqa, a Palestine Liberation Organization (PLO) faction favored by the Syrians, openly strutted through the streets of Damascus ghetto, intimidating people with arms and beatings. Al Fatah also maintained an office in this ghetto where in one week in 1971 seven Jewish homes were torched.[39]

The overall situation was so critical that the Jewish Telegraph Agency of November 19, 1971 reported:

For the first time since the Russian Revolution of 1917, Soviet Jews have petitioned their government to aid Jews of another country. Russian Jewish sources reported that a group of Muscovite Jews wrote to the Kremlin's Big Three—Communist Party chief Leonid I. Brezhnev, Premier Aleksei N. Kosygin, and President Nikolai V. Podgorny—to intervene with the Damascus government for a cessation of restrictions on Syrian Jews. The names of the petitioners were not disclosed, but the sources said they were all activists Jews, many of whom have applied for migration to Israel. The petitioners based their appeal on humanitarian grounds and on the fact of good Russian-Syrian relations.[40]

Highly sensitive to world opinion, Assad's government responded with an orchestrated media blitz of its own. On May 7, 1971, the French weekly *La tribune des nations* published an article on Syrian Jewry by Pierre Demeron. Photographs showed Jews (old and young) raising the fringes of their *tallithim* (prayer shawls) as they gathered in synagogue. Two young women teachers smiled outside the Alliance school while a dozen children cavorted on the beach where they usually picnicked with Muslims and Christians. Another picture showed the opulent copperwares in the Omayad bazaar "owned by the Jewish family of Nasiri." As Demeron interviewed Jewish residents of Damascus, it was clear that they were quite content with their lot.[41]

This was no ghetto. "If we prefer to live in this quarter," explained Selim Totah, the head of the Jewish community, "it is because we have our synagogues, our schools, and above all our kosher shops." The Jewish quarter counted several lawyers, doctors, dentists, and chemists "who practice without any inconvenience or problem."[42] Four hundred children attended schools where they could learn their holy scriptures and where "there are no fights among Jewish, Christian and Moslem children."[43] According to Demeron, Jewish students who received subsidies from abroad were attending all phases of universities. If Jews were obliged to carry specific identity cards it was that "all over the world red ink is used to draw attention at once to an important point."[44] If they were unable to travel freely, it was because a state of war existed with Israel. As Totah pointed out, "You know that this country houses hundreds of thousands of victims of Zionism of whom many are armed and share in the resistance movements. It is no doubt possible that they include among them some who do not differentiate between Jews and Zionists. This measure is not meant to annoy us, but to protect us."[45]

One of the first Western journalists to obtain an interview with Assad, Demeron was told that the Syrian president was going to receive a delegation of Jewish citizens to hear their complaints, "as I have heard those of other classes of citizens." The fight, Assad said, "is for the liberation of all Palestinian Arabs, be they Moslems, Christians or Jews."[46]

Assad apparently was able to dupe others into believing that the old, bad ways in Syria had changed. On January 5, 1975, *New York Times* correspondent Seymour Topping offered the American public a rare view of the lives of Syrian Jews. After rhapsodizing characteristically about "synagogues still being open" and giving the anodyne explanation of official hostility to Jews being due to the technical state of war that made it impossible for Jews to leave the city or country, Topping ended with a conventional stereotype. "The most popular men's clothing store in Damascus is owned by a Jew. 'He is a friend of mine,' said Dr. Saber Falhout, editor of the leading newspaper, Al Baath. 'This suit I am wearing was made by him.' It was a well-tailored plaid."[47]

Shortly after this misleading piece appeared, Topping spent some time with George Gruen of the American Jewish Committee (AJC). Topping was informed that the people he interviewed were among the few Jewish families permitted to function outside ghetto walls, where foreign visitors were taken to display the government's benevolence. Like Demeron, he had spoken with the seventy-year-old Totah and Joseph Jejati, a prominent Jewish merchant; these two trustworthy state appointees lived in comfortable villas and could be counted on to say the right thing for Syria's image abroad.

Topping's report mirrored the findings of another respected Western journalist. Early in 1974, Mike Wallace, a correspondent generally respected for his accuracy, noted on his "At Large" CBS radio show that times had changed since the horrid moment when the Syrians, "a proud people," publicly executed four Jews on charges of spying for Israel. While all was not yet blissful for Jews in Syria (they could not travel freely about the country, Wallace noted, because "many Syrians lost relatives in the series of wars with Israel"), nevertheless conditions had improved since Assad's accession to power. Jews could run their own schools; they entered universities, tuition free if their grades were good enough; and many were doctors, lawyers, and merchants. There were some minor inconveniences—the identity cards for example—but everyone in Syria was required to have such cards. Jews were free to practice their religion and the synagogues were crowded with young people who seemed relatively content.[48] In fact, Wallace spoke with one young pharmacist from Damascus (in the presence of a representative of the Ministry of Information) who related that while he might feel a kinship for Israel, his loyalties in all past and future wars were with Syria. Asked about Arafat's proposal that Oriental Jews should return to the lands of their ancestors once Palestine was restored, this young man innocently responded, "Why not? It would be good to see many of my old friends again. They would be welcome."

Subsequently, a Wallace segment on *60 Minutes* in 1975 would paint an equally misleading picture of conditions in Syria. Once more, carefully selected spokesmen expressed gratitude to the Ba'athist regime for bringing stability to their lives. One, Maurice Nuseyri, owner of that very bazaar celebrated in Demeron's article, offered his own identity card as evidence of a thaw in Arab-Jewish relations. Although there was a line where Nuseyri's religion was typed, the hateful *Mussawi* was lacking. Wallace did inquire how long Nuseyri had had the card, but did not follow up when the latter responded, "Oh, about one week." Nor did the normally relentless journalist inquire after two of Nuseyri's children who had fled the country, abandoning all property in their quest for freedom.[49]

One other prestigious institution would fall victim to Syrian propaganda. The *National Geographic* devoted part of its April, 1974 issue to Syria. An article written by free-lance journalist Robert Azzi told of the "freedom of worship and freedom of opportunity" enjoyed by Syrian Jews, especially in Damascus, "the city still tolerantly (embracing) [sic] significant numbers of Jews."[50] Seven months later, the editors of the *National Geographic,* noting the difficulty of obtaining "reliable, nonpartisan information," tried to swallow Azzi's words.

Many of our Jewish members sharply criticized us for not delineating in greater detail the harsh conditions under which that small community has been forced to exist since 1948. We began to wonder if we had unwittingly failed to reflect the true situation. Now, after months of carefully reviewing the evidence, we have concluded that our critics were right. We erred.[51]

For the first time in its eighty-six years of publication, the *National Geographic* retracted a major article. The evidence that Jews in Syria were not being treated fairly was compelling. Although the Assad government attempted to befog the issue, persecution of Jews continued through the remainder of the decade. What happened to Lillian Abadi and her family and the testimonies offered on these pages by Jews who managed to escape from Syria reflect not some "humanitarian" concern on the part of the Assad government and leaders of the free world, but decades of scorn and derision, coupled with international indifference. Haim Cohn, presiding justice in the Eichmann trial, summed it all up when he said of Syria's Jews, "Their plight is more serious than that of any other Jewish population in the world, but few people seem to be upset by it. Perhaps they're just unaware of how grave the problem is or think the number of Jews in Syria is insignificant compared with the millions who are oppressed elsewhere."[52]

4

The Deal Debating Society

Deal, New Jersey, is located twenty miles south of Fort Monmouth and the Red Bank army arsenal. Nestled between Asbury Park and Long Branch, Deal is one of dozens of boardwalk communities off the Garden State Parkway that have long appealed as summer retreats. For eighty years, New Yorkers have escaped to Luna Parks, seafood inns, condos, health spas, and souvenir stands in towns such as Neptune, Ocean Grove, Avon by the Sea, and Spring Lake.

Few of those hamlets have retained the elegance of Deal, with its great houses—some constructed from pink stucco, others reminiscent of the Vanderbilt retreats at Newport, and still others with their angular wooden frames lifted from the pages of *American Home*. Not even gaudy stone lions, porpoises, or swordfish can lower the average cost ($760,000, making Deal the eleventh costliest neighborhood in the United States according to the Relo Broker Network) of one of these well-trimmed 300-foot lots.[1]

Tourists bound for the nearby racetrack at Long Branch or the casinos of Atlantic City might wonder, but never realize, why this little town slumbers on Saturday afternoons. The clues are there in the town center—the Chocolate Soda restaurant, separate fish and meat markets, a store called the Mitzvah Mart, modestly dressed girls, and bearded men rushing along treed boulevards to the nine synagogues, two Ashkenazic, seven Sephardic, and all Orthodox.

Nearly 700 Jewish families reside in Deal, most of them of Syrian extraction.[2] Descendants of the first immigrants who came to the United States at the turn of the century, they followed the Ashkenazim from the ghettos of Brooklyn as their economic lot improved, seeking fresh sea breezes. Only they did not come as summer transients. They bought homes, put down roots, built yeshivas, yet never severed their ties with the larger Syrian community in Ocean Parkway. To this day, every weekday, three buses filled with Syrian Jewish commuters make the 150-mile loop to businesses in Brooklyn.

On a Saturday afternoon in the fall of 1986 when I drove into Deal, there were no televisions turned to college football games. Instead, men and women remained in their synagogues, studying with their rabbis until the evening prayers. A huge, old mansion surrounded by high hedges serves as synagogue and home for Rabbi Isaac F. and his congregation. It is a makeshift arrangement—the ark and bimah (reading platform) situated in a parlor with folding chairs. An eerie experience for the offspring of European Jews to hear the near-Arabic singsong of Sephardic Hebrew chanted by men who otherwise speak perfect Brooklynese.

When services were over, I was invited to share the Shabbat Seudah meal of tuna, melons, rolls, and Dewar's scotch. Before the rabbi, himself a refugee from Aleppo, broke into his *nigunim* (Chasidic songs) discussion among the twenty men and boys assembled at the dining room table focused on the recent massacre of Jews in Istanbul. Theories flew back and forth as to whether such acts of violence were directed at Jews as such or were intended to dislodge Israel from occupied territories. As the discussion became less fervid, the rabbi introduced me, noting that I was researching a book on Syrian Jewry. Once more the group became animated, and the exchange went something like this.[3]

"I hope you're not going to put down the Arabs." The speaker was a rotund, crewcut gentleman in his sixties. "They're not so bad. I lived with them and they didn't bother us."

He was interrupted by a second man who was bald and had a large nose. "Yeah, but you left in 1941. That's not the situation today."

"There is no persecution today," responded the first man. "People have it good. No one is dying or being tortured."

At this point, Rabbi Isaac F. reminded everyone that Syrian Jews were not free to emigrate. I added that a recent report of Amnesty International cited a number of human rights abuses (long-term detention without trial, summary procedures, "disappearances") under provisions of Syria's state of emergency, which had been in force since 1963. While omitting any reference to the plight of Jews, Amnesty International cited 200 prisoners of conscience (mostly communist, Kurdish nationalists, and former government ministers) who, along with other prisoners in Syria's jails, were being subjected routinely to torture.[4]

"I was just there." The voice was that of nineteen-year-old Benjamin Z., formerly of Damascus and now a premed student at Yeshiva University. "From time to time the Syrian government makes new decisions. Sometimes they say you're allowed to sell your house. Then in two, three months, you're not allowed to sell your house without permission. They announce the new rules to the community. It's bad. You can't move. You can't sell your property."

"Neither could I," said the man with the crewcut.

"That's not persecution?" asked the second man.

Benjamin responded, "You couldn't buy things. You're constantly in fear.

Palestinians came in and took homes among the Jews. The Jews over there are gathered in one place, like here in Deal, a small place, four or five thousand Jews. Old streets and houses. If any Palestinian is going to hit you, you can't say anything, because you're afraid. He's a Palestinian. You're a Jew. The secret police are responsible for the Jews. Nobody can touch them. They deal with the person who wants to escape just like a spy."

"That's just ash-Shams [Damascus], not Halab [Aleppo] or Al-Qāmishlī," said the first man, munching on half a cantaloupe. "Of course the Syrians have to keep track of the Jews. We're a minority. There could be espionage."

"We have minorities and don't keep them under constant surveillance. Blacks, Mexicans." The voice was that of a fourth, elderly Jew wearing an embroidered skullcap.

"It's policy," insisted the first man.

"You mean politics," added the second.

"No, policy."

"Just like the difference between bad Zionists and good Jews," said the second.

"Perhaps a fairer comparison can be made between Syria's Jews and those of Nazi Germany in the 1930s," I offered.

"I don't agree. The situations are different. Jews and Arabs are pretty much alike. It's just religion. There's no gassing." The swarthy, paunchy man in his thirties who made these remarks had amassed a fortune retailing toys and games in Brooklyn. Turning to the student, he asked, "Tell me. How many do you think would leave if given a chance?"

"Probably fifty to sixty percent," interrupted the man with the skullcap.

"I don't know," said the student. "Probably most of them would."

"What about Mrs. Abadi?" asked the toy salesman.

"That had nothing to do with being Jewish," snapped the first man. "He owed money and wouldn't pay it."

At this point, the rabbi turned to the same man (who was old enough to be his father) and spoke. "Let me ask you. If you have a bird and keep it in a cage, the best cage, give it the best food, is that bird free?"

There was no reply from any of the sages in Deal.

Later, I sat and talked with the rabbi who had fled his home city of Aleppo at the age of seventeen in 1970. A bearded, young-looking man with a hawk nose and blue eyes, he quietly explained why the Syrians are reluctant to let Jews emigrate.

"I'm not a prophet on the percentages that would emigrate, but I am sure that everyone has someone outside of Syria they would like to see—parents, brothers, sisters, grandparents. They'd like to meet with each other. I think one of the reasons they don't want Jews to come to Israel I heard once from one of the *Muhabarat*. 'If you let these families, all the young boys, go to Israel, they're going to be in the army. And we believe that every Israeli soldier is worth one hundred Syrians. If we prevent Jews from going to Israel, our army will be stronger.' That's also why the PLO doesn't bomb outside of Israel, because they don't want to scare the Jews in the Diaspora to start moving to Israel. So all the bombs on buses and places in Israel are just to run the Jews away from their homeland, from Israel outside. The main leadership of the PLO camp, I think, doesn't agree with terror like that in Istanbul. Still, they're confusing all the Jewish people inside Israel and out.''[5]

American writer Lynn Simarski has lavished praise on Aleppo, Syria's commercial center, an ancient city of "polychrome inlaid marble," "elegant courtyards," "citrus trees, jasmine, and roses grow[ing] in basins near fountains or pools," and a *suq* (market) "sometimes called the most beautiful in the entire Middle East."[6] Why had Rabbi Isaac F. decided to flee such an idyllic scene?

"Do you remember what happened in Aleppo in 1947? They came and burned the shuls and stores, even my father's store. They came to burn his store and a miracle happened. Above his store was a balcony. The stones fell from the balcony, so the Arabs were afraid. They said, 'Oh, this balcony is going to fall down on us. So we'll leave this store and go to the next one.' It was an old building and at the entrance a piece of stone fell from this balcony right in front of the store. So they grew frightened and ran away. When they came to my grandmother's house, they walked in the shuls, burned the Torahs.

"Then every time they had a war with Israel, 1967, 1973, many Arabs were killed. Somebody's brother, uncle. And afterwards, they used to bring the dead Arabs back. If it was a regular soldier, they used to leave him in the field. They didn't bring them back to the house. But if he was a captain or some important person, they would bring him and leave the dead body right in front, knock on the door, and leave. They wouldn't talk—nothing. The family opens and sees a body bag or box, the father or the son. They take care of the body, but they want to take revenge on somebody, and they have no one else but us. It happened to one of our neighbors in 1967. We lived very close to them. After, they looked at us as enemies. One of my family may have killed one of his family, his father. They knew we had relatives in Israel.''

Syria's disastrous performance in the Six Day War of June 1967 had more immediate repercussions for the Jews of Aleppo. Isaac's father, a lawyer, was disbarred. Under rules of a curfew, no one was permitted beyond their own porch after sunset. One woman who went into the street had her head shaved. Another man who went out for bread was taken to police headquarters and beaten.

"Sometimes people put into effect rules that didn't come from Damascus. The *goyim* (Gentiles) threw rocks at people going to shul. The Arab kids had fights with us. If you went to the police, they would say, 'You're the bad guys,' the Jews. You can do nothing. One time, when I was twelve or thirteen years old, they threw a stone at me. It hit here, on my head. I had to go to the hospital for some stitches. You can still see the mark. They called us *Yahud, Mussawi*. In the third- and fourth-grade textbooks, they have 'You don't have any enemies but the Jews.' They teach that and we have to read that. We also had to read the Quran. It's not true there is no anti-Semitism in the Quran. I used to know the Sura of the Table, Imrams, Woman, Cow. It encourages people to commit suicide jihad, just to save their own people. They would stop us on the streets, hold you in a corner with both hands at your side, and force you to say: 'Muhammad is God's true prophet.' We used to say it, but in a funny, fast way so it didn't mean the right thing.''

Isaac's dissatisfaction with life in Syria (''you have no future . . . all the time you are afraid somebody's following you . . . it happened to me for about six months after I left the country'') apparently became obvious even to the *Muhabarat,* which tried to entrap him as a teenager.

''When I was seventeen years old, they [the *Muhabarat*] offered to smuggle me out. My father was very involved with the *Muhabarat.* They were located right in the middle of the ghetto next to our house and the post office. A modern two-story stone building. No guards, nothing in front. Any question, they would ask my father—like a *mukhtar* [village chieftain]. When we had a problem, they would call him to the *Muhabarat* and question him. So he had a little confidence talking to them.

''They used to come to us. One time, two of them, about twenty-four and twenty-six years old, came to me and my friend and said, 'Why don't you come with us to visit Lebanon?' I told him we are Jewish people and aren't even allowed to leave Aleppo. He said, 'No problem. I'll try to arrange something.' They wanted to trap us. This way would create fear among Jews so that if any real smugglers came they wouldn't run away with them.

''The one man was named Mahmud. He was friendly to us. The other was named Massoud and he was really mean. I used to drive a motorcycle, go around like all teenagers, showing off. Then one time, they started coming. They knew we were Jews. They said, 'Let's see whose bike is better.' I said, 'Look, your motorcycle is bigger than mine. If you give it to me, I'm sure I would win.' I didn't know the guy. Both were contacts for the *Muhabarat.* We followed them once after work. I told my friend Nahum, 'Let's see where they're going.' They were from the *Muhabarat.*

''We were four boys at the time, just finishing high school. It happened that the other two boys got scared and said, 'We don't want to deal with them.' So the two of us said right now we're not doing anything illegal. We'll give them some information and see. I told them we'll go out for a trip to see if the way is clear to Lebanon, and come back. First, let's see if there's no problem. They brought a map and started to explain to us how we could leave Syria for Lebanon.

''We didn't trust them one hundred percent. We started asking other Arabs who were smuggling back and forth to Lebanon for different reasons (drugs or other stuff). We found that the road was pretty safe, that we could go by ourselves. We decided to take a shot, to go without them. When they came to us one day, I told them, 'Listen, my father heard that we are going outside Syria with you and he is going to tell the *Muhabarat.* So, please, we would like to go with you, but not now. We're going to postpone a little while, let things cool off, and then we'll go.' It happens they convinced one of my friends to run away. They caught him in the middle of the road at Hama. A trap. When you hear your friend has been caught, you get scared. You have to watch very carefully not to be trapped like him.''

What Isaac and his friend Nahum did seems reckless enough. "We had to do all kinds of different things to run away. We had to get non-Jewish identity cards. You can't change a Jewish ID card because they have *Mussawi* written across. They're laminated. We went to a place where they exercise, a health club, people changing clothes. We used to go there often, monthly. We had to get three ID cards, one for me, one for my friend, and one for practice. We took off the pictures of the goy and put on our own. We went to one of the quick photos. You have to know which kind of picture. Not a glossy, the other kind. It's easy to put a stamp on it. You have to find the right shape for the stamp, a bottle top to complete the circle of the picture. Then you have to put Arabic on top—Syrian Arab Republic. We changed the names because if the goy reported his ID card lost, they would check at the border. So we had to change the name and number of each person. For example, the name might be Mustapha, so you put Abul Hassan. We had to erase the whole thing, experiment with different combinations so when you erased you wouldn't leave a different color on the identity card. The paper had to be the same. The card had to be in plastic, so you removed the plastic by heating it with an iron. That's the way the plastic was applied, so you removed it by heat. That's what you learn in the Torah. Everything can be koshered by heat. To remove *hometz* or *treyf,* remove it by boiling heat.

"So we got one card from the health club and one from the library. In Syria, when you go to the library, you put your ID card in a box. We saw a man with a thick book. It would take him forever to read. We took his card, ran all the way, and hid in a building. We did it in the basement of somebody's house. Nobody knew about it. Then we waited a week and started out.

"Just as in the Torah, it says God told Abraham to leave the town and country with his family and go to the Promised Land that he did not know, that's exactly what happened to us. We left and didn't tell our parents, our family, and we came to Lebanon. We had nobody in Lebanon, but we felt we had a better chance to get to America that way. We changed clothes, like a farmer, an Arab *fellah,* and walked. If they saw us, they wouldn't see two students. We didn't want them to think we were Jews. We didn't take *tzitzit* [undershirt with fringes worn by religious Jews] or *yarmulkes* [skullcaps] with us, not even food. It was Ramadan at the time.

"So we walked. At the border there were two checkpoints, one Syrian, one Lebanese. We had to run away from the Syrian because if they asked for our passports, we didn't have any. If the Syrians stopped us, we would have been sent directly to jail. There was a village, the last village before the border. Instead of going along the road, we went off and made a big detour, avoiding the Syrian checkpoint through the mountains and desert. When we came to the Lebanese checkpoint, we gave the identity cards with the changed pictures and names. They looked. One is named Hamad, the other Abu Ali. Then they gave us entry permits which were legal for Lebanon and we walked in.''[7]

Isaac and Nahum had simply walked away one day after school without telling anyone. Back home, their departure caused a sensation. "The Arabs [from the *Muhabarat*] came back and heard we'd left. My parents were scared. They had to go every night to tell the police that one of the children hadn't come home. They weren't looking for trouble. The police told my father, 'It's your fault.' He said, 'It's not my fault. Give me a car and I'll go to Turkey and look for him and bring him back.' He was lucky they didn't give him a hard time. After two or three days of interrogation, they sent him back home.''[8]

Eventually, the families in Aleppo received a telegram: "Twins born in Beirut. Mazl tov. Isaac/Nahum." When the cable passed through *Muhabarat* offices, "they didn't make a big thing out of it." Says Rabbi F., "They said, 'Oh, it's nothing. We'll pass it along.' " Later, in Beirut, Isaac F. encountered the police informer Mahmud. "He told me that after we left Syria, they put our pictures up everywhere. 'Whoever finds these two boys will receive a big reward.' They put his other friend in prison for a while because they claimed he was the one who helped us run away. The *Muhabarat* thought they took money from us. They couldn't believe that seventeen-year-olds could do everything by themselves.''

In Beirut, the boys sought assistance from what was then a fairly prosperous Jewish community numbering 8,000. "They were very suspicious," says Rabbi Isaac. "They didn't want to accept us at first. They thought we were *goyim* doing the same thing [entrapment for the *Muhabarat*], especially when they saw our identity cards.'' One man who actively intervened on their behalf was Albert Elia, the Lebanese Jewish leader who was kidnapped and (presumably) killed in 1971. "He had a big hand in helping us," says Rabbi Isaac. "Elia disappeared right after we arrived.''

The rabbi did not see his parents again for fourteen years. One by one, his nine siblings managed to escape ("to Israel, America, it didn't matter where they went, just to get out of there") and each time his father weas imprisoned for two weeks. In 1984, with one brother ailing in Switzerland, the parents, too, were permitted to leave Syria.

"First, we brought my mother out. We sent my brother to Switzerland with a letter from a doctor and sent that to the *Muhabarat* telling them the boy had to have an operation. They didn't know he was living in Israel. It would only make them angry. When we saw one another for the first time, we embraced and cried. For weeks and days our eyes would mist over.''

Rabbi Isaac F. is married to an American woman and is the father of two beautiful children. He instructs novices in the ways of Sephardic, Orthodox Judaism; supports the day schools in Deal; and presses his congregants for *tzedakah* (charity) for seminaries in Israel. One of his brothers is studying for the rabbinate in Jerusalem. His parents now live in a settlement in Bat Yam. And yet his story lacks resolution.

"*Baruch hashem* [thank God]. All of my family are out, but one. My second oldest brother is still there. He had a bad experience. He tried to escape and they caught him. On the way to the Turkish border, his father-in-law passed away. A terrible thing. They put my brother in jail for four to six months. And to be in a Syrian jail, I don't wish for anybody to be there. My father was in a few times for helping people get out of Syria, getting passports in a legal way. But they gave him a hard time."

There are problems for those who managed to escape. The rabbi is critical of what he perceives to be inadequacies and insensitivity in Israel's absorption process. "My father is doing nothing in Israel. It's very difficult to find a job, especially when he doesn't know the language. He's a man who worked years and years to help people coming out. His Arabic is very good. He knows some French. They could give him a job with the Ministry of Education. The *Sochnut* [Jewish Agency] should contact him and try to help.[9]

"When I visited the Gilo absorption center, there was a family that came from Qāmishlī. Qāmishlī is not a place with a high standard of living. But people were sitting on the floor in winter. Winters in Israel are not like they are here, freezing. But you're better prepared for the cold weather here. In Israel, if you don't have something, it's very hard. You can get sick. I went with a few friends of mine and collected three to four hundred dollars, bought six or eight families silverware, carpets, chairs, because some had only cartons or boxes to sit on.

"I know it's very hard and the people of the *Sochnut* lose patience because they see so many people. If you work steadily on a job for years, you get tired of it. It becomes routine. Even people who work in a cemetery, God forbid, they do it every day so it has no feeling. I think you have to work at these places only for a short time. That way you'll have better feelings toward the *Olim Hadashim* [new immigrants]. Not just the people from Syria, but everywhere. Once a boy told them, 'If this is the way you will treat me, I'm going back to Syria.' So they said, 'You go. Who's holding you? Go back!' That's not the way. If he's telling you something like that, he's crying from the inside. Something is bothering him."

Rabbi Isaac F. is equally outspoken about those members of his own debating society who equivocate or counsel timid gestures on behalf of Jews still trapped in Syria. "You can't compare the Jewish quarter there with what we have here," he said. "I was reading an article that said there were seventy-four anti-Semitic acts in all of New Jersey this year. They're calling for the people to be aware. As for Syria, I think every time we write something, the government there cares. The *Muhabarat* tells people who go to the States to say something good about us." Then echoing his metaphor about a bird in a gilded cage, he told me, "It's said that if a child won't cry, his mother won't feed it. If you keep quiet and the world knows nothing about it, they can do the same thing. Only next time, it will be worse and worse."

5

Sophie's Choice

September, 1986. It is seventy miles from the plush homes of Deal to the slums of Williamsburg. A pathetic odyssey brought Orli Gamaliel and her family from their home in Al-Qāmishlī to this once elegant section of Brooklyn. Immigrants fleeing the congestion of Delancey Street in Lower Manhattan must have been enthralled by the rustic atmosphere in Williamsburg at one time. Some of the old splendor remains on Broadway and Myrtle avenue—huge, domed banks, churches, and synagogues. But only a few yards from the overhead M or J transit, there are pawnshops, taco stands, and endless rows of abandoned brick tenements. Every window is gutted; graffiti are sprayed in Spanish or the puzzling "Fuck the 90%. Dead Eye." Says one of the residents, "As buildings go down, the rats move into the next building."[1] It is a depressing sight, one reminiscent of Berlin in 1945, and it is also ironic, because busloads of German and Japanese tourists pass by to seek a glimpse of what fabled Brooklyn looks like today.

There are a few public housing towers, which blot out the East River, and a few concrete zones to which bewigged Jewish matrons trundle their babies for recreation. For despite its trash, broken bottles, and high crime rate, Williamsburg persists as one of the last Jewish enclaves in north Brooklyn. The Satmarer Chasidim, a pietistic sect that traces its roots to Hungary,[2] has nestled into this squalid region. The Satmarers run kosher delis, peddle every conceivable head covering from fancy fur *shtreiml* to sedate homburg, and maintain a number of educational institutions where ear-curled children imbide anti-Zionism. They were also responsible for bringing Orli Gamaliel to her two-bedroom basement flat.

Unlike her husband, Ezra, who has yet to master English since coming to the United States in 1980, Orli Gamaliel has developed a good command of her adopted tongue. A captivating woman, her blue eyes glow when she speaks lovingly of her four children: Rima, born in Al-Qāmishlī and only recently back from a visit to friends in Toronto; Nora, a wide-eyed little girl born in 1974; Gabi, the one son, born in 1975; and Fuleh, born in Syria in 1977, a radiant child who gives new meaning to the phrase "raven-haired beauty."

The Gamaliel family resides not so much in an apartment as a cluster of basement rooms connected by a long hallway, which government rent control fixes at $320 per month. The two oldest girls sleep on living room sofas. The children are growing up bilingually (Arabic and Yiddish, no English) under the strict supervision of the Satmarers. The family has a television set, but it is hidden away in the parents' room under a drape because this Chasidic sect considers television a sinful medium. Recently, Rima lamented to her mother, "I can't live like this, long stockings in the summer, my hair in a bun. I'll go crazy." Even worse, the youngest girl was terrified when she walked into the bathroom in the middle of the night and saw a rat. Mrs. Gamaliel says, "I must live in a place where my child is afraid to go to the bathroom at night?"[3]

Mrs. Gamaliel has friends in Israel who would welcome her, but she cannot bring herself to face them. "They remember how I used to be," she says. "How when we lived in Qāmishlī, I used to be so happy, dance, sing, until I was twenty-seven. Now it's all different."

Orli and her family lived in that small town in the northeast corner of Syria where her husband worked in a shoe store and she taught kindergarten to Jewish children. Her parents and several relatives moved to Aleppo in 1967. Then in 1978, like so many others who found life in Syria unbearable, the Gamaliels decided to escape. "It was very hard for people in Qāmishlī because of the *Muhabarat*. The *Muhabarat* in Qāmishlī is harder than in Aleppo or Damascus. Terrible people. You live here with the *Muhabarat* upstairs, this side, that side. You cannot listen to Israel radio. Big shots. You feel they are watching you.

"If it's a good place, you don't want to leave. But if you have to watch behind you all the time, everyone will want to go. There was no freedom. Now people are allowed to go out with passports. Not then. I believe some people in Damascus would not leave even now because they would have to leave everything, stores, furniture. There are a few very rich. But not in Qāmishlī. They are very poor."

One day in 1978, an Arab woman who was a neighbor approached the Gamaliels and informed them she had been to Turkey and was bearing a letter from a brother who had fled to that country several years before. If the Gamaliels wished to escape, the woman was willing to serve (at a price) as intermediary with smugglers who had taken two groups across the border. At first, the Gamaliels did not offer any encouragement. "In truth," says Orli, "we were afraid and told her we don't want any letter from a brother and don't wish to escape."

The woman returned with a Jewish man who assured them he knew her very well and could vouch for her integrity. The test of her reliability came, however, when another Jewish woman, fleeing with seven children, informed Orli she would send back a necklace open at the clasp and a white handkerchief if everything went well with her crossing. If she sent a red handkerchief instead, it would represent a warning. "When we received the necklace and the white handkerchief," Orli recounted, "I told my sister the same thing, 'If it's all right, I will send the open necklace.' "

There were twenty-nine people in the Gamaliel's party, including four children ranging in age from nine months to six years, Mr. Gamaliel's brother and a daughter, plus two other families. Orli recalls that night in October, 1978. "Each adult had to pay three thousand Syrian liras. That's about five hundred dollars. For the children, it was more—forty-five hundred liras because it was more dangerous. We had to get sleeping pills. Nobody gave us notice the day we escaped. We didn't meet at one place. I told people I was going to my sister's. My husband came from work. We were picked up in a big truck driven by the Arab woman's husband about 8:00 P.M. The truck stopped at different places, corners where people were standing. Nobody paid any attention.

"The driver took us to a village about twenty miles outside town. He put everybody down where the four smugglers were waiting. We weren't at the border yet. We started walking. It was very dark. There was no moon. It was very hard to go walking in the mountains at night carrying the sleeping children on our backs.

"We were gone about thirty minutes when suddenly two cars came driving up full of uniformed soldiers. Then another two cars. One hundred men surrounded us. The Arab woman had betrayed us. She had heard the *Muhabarat* was paying a reward for turning in Jews. So after she received her money from us, she got more from the *Muhabarat*.

"The smugglers told us to lie down. Then shooting started. It must have gone on for twenty minutes because the soldiers opened fire on us and the smugglers, who had guns, started shooting back. The *Muhabarat* shone their car lights on us and the shooting continued like rain over our heads. All the children began to cry and we were all shouting, 'We're not going! Please! Stop shooting!' Then my four-year-old daughter started crying. She stood up and started running because she was so frightened. I got up from the ground to bring her back. The *Muhabarat* saw me by the lights of the cars and shot me."

Orli was not the only one who was wounded. One of the smugglers who had been hit in the leg was abandoned as his three companions ran to safety. He would spend a year in a Syrian prison. Mrs. Gamaliel's wounds, however, were far more serious. She recalled, "One shot hit my kidney and other hit my spine. The instant I was shot, I could not move my legs, and I was bleeding from my back. I fell on my daughter, and even the *Muhabarat* did not know who was hit, my daughter or I, because my daughter was covered from my own bleeding."

In the official report of the *Muhabarat*, Mrs. Gamaliel was shot while "escaping to Israel." (It is over 400 miles from Qāmishlī to the Golan Heights.) More important, the two rifle bullets that entered her left side did extensive internal damage before exiting from the right of her spine. Doctors who examined her at the Qāmishlī hospital took one look at the gaping three-inch tear in her back and dismissed her, saying, "She will be dead in three hours."

Still conscious, Orli begged the *Muhabarat* to bring her sister before she died. "I thought I was going to die and asked her to take care of my children as if they were her own." Orli's sister started screaming, insisting that the police take her to Aleppo where the rest of the family lived. The trip took nine hours by ambulance and when Mrs. Gamaliel was brought to the hospital Syrian doctors again refused to treat her. They said, "Let her die so that every Jew will know and stay where he is and not attempt to escape."

Fortunately for Mrs. Gamaliel, a Jewish doctor, Musa Antaby, intervened. Dr. Antaby (coincidentally Victor Abadi's brother-in-law) secured a blood transfusion from one of Orli's relatives, then performed an eight-hour operation on her spine. From that day, Orli has been paralyzed from the waist down. "I remained twenty-six days without any memory and without recognizing anyone. After that, the doctors released me from the hospital and I stayed at my sister's house. For the next nine months, I was just like a baby. I could not move because my back and my left side was open. All day long, my brothers had to move me from side to side. My urinary tract and colon were burned and I was moaning and crying. I had no sensation in the lower part of my body and was like an infant. My sister had to clean me as you would an infant. This was a bitter time—severe pain for twenty-four hours a day. I said every moment, 'I don't want this life. I want to die, even if I have four children. I can't even control myself.' "

After a year in Aleppo, the *Muhabarat* permitted Orli to travel to Italy for medical treatment. She was accompanied by her mother and father who then returned to Syria. With the aid of the Israeli consul in Rome, Orli continued on to a hospital in Jerusalem. In the next sixteen months, she underwent three more operations to close the wounds of her back. She had not seen her husband or children since the betrayal at the border. What news she did receive was grave.

"After the first escape attempt, my husband was taken to jail for three months. I didn't even know if he was alive. Every day he was hungry. Every day they used to torture him by binding him and flogging and punching him. Four men used to throw him from one wall to another, like a ball one throws him to the other. They beat him on the back and feet. To this day, his feet ache him continuously.

"During the time I was in Israel, my husband left prison and tried once more to escape with my four children, five brothers, my sister, and her husband. One family had seven children, another four. They tried sleeping pills on the children, but they didn't work. A baby (one of my brother's) cried, revealing their position. They had walked five hours and now they were arrested and forced to walk back. They hit the men with rifle butts on the way back, in front of the children. That's the way the *Muhabarat* would act. They tortured the father in front of the son. My father was arrested six times. The *Muhabarat* took my grandfather with him, and for one month they tortured him in front of my grandfather. My father is sixty-two years old, lame, blind in one eye and suffering hearing loss in one ear from so many beatings at the hands of the *Muhabarat*. The children were crying all the way, seeing the *Muhabarat* beating their parents. They were screaming and crying, but no mercy was shown.

"My husband and my brothers and my brother-in-law were imprisoned for six months. They transferred them from the Damascus prison to one in Aleppo in an open truck in the bitter cold. There were thirty-eight people in one room and they slept on the floor. Thirty-eight men in a little cell with only one bathroom. It smelled so bad. The blankets they gave them were full of lice. Their bodies were itching, bleeding badly.

"They tortured them every day and their torture was very severe. My youngest brother was thirteen years old. Four men used to slap him until he fainted. My second brother was twenty-one years old and almost lost his eyesight from the severe beatings. He suffered a detached retina and was blindfolded for days. The injury had to be corrected by surgery in the U.S. Four different men hit my husband. They knocked him down a flight of stairs and the men hit from one to the other to the other. They tied him inside a great tire and used electric wire—shocks—on him."[4]

Fearing for the safety of Orli's husband and children should the *Muhabarat* discover she was in Israel, authorities in that country sent her to the Kingsbrook Medical Center in New York. From there it was only a matter of time and insensitivity before she came to Williamsburg. "I was two months in the hospital when someone came from the consulate and said they wouldn't pay anymore. I must return to Israel. I didn't want to go. 'They'll kill my husband and five brothers if they find out.' I was taken from the hospital by a *Bikur Holim* (social service) volunteer to a convalescent home for the aged. Everyone was ninety or one hundred. I was in that home two or three days, crying all day. I didn't eat anything. Only some tea with a piece of bread, the kind of food, soup, they give old people. But I was a young woman, twenty-seven. The nurse said, 'Don't cry.' But I want to; go to my family. Finally a man, Mr. Landau, a driver for the home, helped me. He was a Satmarer. He took me to Williamsburg, found my apartment, got food, started me on my green card. Then my neighbor Mr. Gross helped out, got me a Medicaid card from the city, welfare, and a red card to park anywhere. The car, a 1980 Chevrolet with handicapped shift and a special device to pickup a wheelchair came from my friend, Mrs. Judy, in Canada.

"For two years, I was living in this place by myself, with these walls. I lived with no one. No friends or acquaintance. If I wanted to get out to the street, I had to wait until somebody rang the doorbell, so they could help me up the stairs. Or else I had to crawl up on my hands and knees, even in the snow and rain. I tried a ramp, but I slid into the wall. For two years, I would talk to myself like a crazy person. I used to look at my children's picture and talk to them and kiss the picture. I used to cry all the time and my tears flowed like a river. Those were horrible days and cruel nights."

During that period, Orli made a host of appeals on behalf of her family. She went to the United Nations and was reassured by a woman that the office of the secretary general would make confidential inquiries via Geneva. Whenever she called back (every three weeks), Orli was told that the secretary general's office could not give an answer yet. "To this day," she says, "I have received no formal communication."

She traveled to Washington and spoke with officials at the Syrian Embassy, promising to return to her homeland once additional surgery was performed in the United States. Nothing could be done, she was informed, no passports issued. Orli would have to speak directly to the *Muhabarat* in Syria. In desperation, she wrote a letter to President Assad. Plaintively, in Arabic, she explained how she was a simple Syrian citizen, a mother who wanted to see her children one last time before undergoing life-threatening surgery of eight hours at Yale University Medical Center. Attached to the letter was a photograph of the children and records of surgery done at Kingsbrook and Beth Israel hospitals.

Because two years had passed without a response from Assad, the Gamaliel family in Syria pooled its resources, hoping to bribe officials in charge of exit permits. Orli's father, mother, and brothers contributed $1,700 to purchase a diamond necklace for one official. "It was like Atlantic City," she says. "All or nothing at all."

Then, suddenly, Mrs. Gamaliel was informed her husband would receive a travel permit good for thirty days. There was one small problem: thirteen days of that time had already lapsed and the Syrians would not let him go without another deposit of $5,000. Orli called one of the wealthy figures in the Syrian Jewish community in New York not once, but several times. Although the businessman's secretary promised to convey the message, there were no return calls. Later, the same individual remarked, "I can't be troubled with every refugee who comes from Syria."

With only six days left in Mr. Gamaliel's travel permit, the Canadian Committee for the Rescue of Syrian Jewry intervened. "Judy Feld Carr," says Mrs. Gamaliel, "she is an angel. I didn't know her from Adam. But somebody told me to contact them by telephone. I was afraid with her. That same day, the money was wired to Syria."

Any celebrations would have been premature. In Syria, the police were orchestrating a scene straight out of *Sophie's Choice*. "When my husband went to the *Muhabarat,* they told him, 'We know you don't intend to come back after seven days.' He admitted he would try to stay as long as possible. 'I won't lie to you. I'll go to Washington and try to get an extension of two or three months from the consul.' The Syrians screamed and hit him, 'You tried to escape and now you want a passport for all four children, too? You can take only two. When you come back, we will let the other children go.'

"All of them went to the airport with my mother. We decided to have the youngest and oldest stay. What a painful day it was when my husband left two children behind him. Rima, who was seven and one-half, was crying, 'Daddy, now you leave me, too? Isn't it enough Momma left me?' He was crying, 'What will happen to the two children?' ''

Faced with the dilemma of some of them getting out or none, the family decided the eldest and youngest would stay. Rima suposedly could help her grandmother and aunts with the baby who did not understand what was happening anyway. This grim scene was enacted at the same Damascus airport where Lieutenant Goodman was later released by humanitarian Syrian authorities.

"I saw my husband and two children after an absence of two years. But my heart was not completely happy because the other two babies were still in Syria. I received letters from Rima, in the second grade. she wrote, 'Mommy, I miss you.' She touched my heart.

"I continued to get in touch with anyone who could help in their departure, but without success. The two sisters could not even see each other because each of them was in a different town. The small child was with my sister in Qāmishlī and the older one was with my sister in Aleppo.

"After four and one-half years, they were able to get a passport. They also had to pay a deposit, and once again help came from Mrs. Judy. The reunion took place at JFK Airport in July, 1984. My mother, who had a deposit to return to Syria, came with them on Alia, Jordan Air. The big one was excited to see the little one. The two didn't see much of one another. We were so excited, tearful. The girls hugged and embraced one another. Rima said, 'Thank God, I come. But it hurts me a lot to see you in a wheelchair.' The baby didn't know or understand. She asked, 'Why are you in a chair? Why this? Why that?' That night in the apartment, she cried and said she wanted to go home to her mother. She felt my sister who raised her in Aleppo was her mother. It hurt me a lot. She was upset that first day until I took her for a ride on a neighbor's bike. Then her smile flashed.''

How do the children get along now? "Pretty good, not like the neighbors," Mrs. Gamaliel says. "Every now and then there is some jealousy because they feel we are giving something extra to the baby and they may resent it because she no longer is a baby. But they have more love for one another because of what they have experienced. The adjustment is very hard. When I'm shivering with pain in bed, the children feel very bad.''

The children endure their existence in a rat-infested cellar, for there is hope that once they grow up they will leave the stifling atmosphere of Satmarer Williamsburg. Unfortunately, the same cannot be said for their parents. Beatings sustained in Syrian jails have left more than physical scars on Ezra Gamaliel. Outwardly genial to visitors, he sits at home most of the time, in Orli's words, "like a *golem*."[5] Ezra Gamaliel is a man afraid of going into Manhattan to learn English at the offices of NYANA,[6] of going into a nearby Chasidic synagogue to *doven* (pray) lest his style or tone of speech offend someone, and of venturing into the street lest he be condemned as a "damned Zionist" for trying to communicate in Hebrew. Reduced to a *shammes* (custodian) in Syria, he is unable to work here for more than four or five hours daily as an office cleaner. According

to one source, "He is morally broken, scared of his own shadow." In the words
of a sympathetic social worker, "As a result of his torture, he is a dysfunctional
man, totally dependent, like a fifth child." When an older brother recently visited
New York, he marveled about Ezra. "I didn't recognize him. He is twenty years
older than I am. He's a dead man."[7]

Then there is Orli Gamaliel herself, taking twelve to fourteen pills each day,
Tylenol-3, codeine, to kill the pain. Her doctors have suggested pain clinics
from Minnesota to North Carolina, more protracted surgery, none of which will
ever restore feeling below the waist. She wonders why she has to shave her hair
and wear a *sheytl* (wig) to placate the Satmarers, why her children must grow
up as strangers to American culture, why her husband cannot be trained for
useful employment, why they must live in a hovel in a deteriorating Ashkenazic
neighborhood, when not so distant is a flourishing Sephardic community. Not
in Deal, New Jersey, but along Ocean Parkway, near Brighton Beach, Benson-
hurst, Coney Island, there are 30,000 of her own people. Only five miles from
the Satmarers, there are ten Sephardic synagogues that average a Saturday attendance of 5,000 people. Every family, without exception, keeps a kosher home.
5,000 children attend Jewish day schools. And, trumpets a statement issued on
the visit of the Israeli prime minister in September, 1986, "In the last five years
in over 400 marriages there has not been one instance of intermarriage—intermarriage is when we marry an Ashkenazi."

"There are so many rich Syrian Jews in New York, Toronto, and I have to
live like this?" asks Orli. "Sometimes I think I will go crazy in this place.
Nobody understands my problems. We have nice neighbors, but when we have
a worker in the house, a black woman, three or four times a week, she asks
how I got hurt and I tell her in an auto accident. Because if I tell her the truth,
I have to answer more questions. I feel so bad. I feel like a movie is before my
eyes when I think about it. I think back on what kind of person I was and now
what I have to do."

Orli Gamaliel adds, "Even though I was shot, I would do it again. The Syrians
keep Jews just as hostages." To which her husband adds, "*Caen. Nachon*
[right]."

November, 1988. When I left the Gamaliel family two years ago, Orli spoke
of the sadness she had for her children and her husband, the fear she felt that
"the Satmarers will smash my windows." According to Judy Carr, the Canadian
woman who helped bring the family out, relocation of the Gamaliels took prec-
edence over every activity related to Syrian Jewry. "Moving that family out of
Williamsburg will be a great mitzvah," she told me. "Saul, if we don't get her
out of there, I'm afraid something dreadful is going to happen."[8]

Somehow, for eight years, the Gamaliels fell between the cracks of bureau-
cratic relief and resettlement programs. The Joint Distribution Committee (JDC)
was aware of their plight, but could do little because its mandate operates beyond

the borders of the United States. Dedicated workers at NYANA were equally frustrated, for here again the emphasis is on education and job training of new immigrants within their first two months of arrival in this country. Chronic cases such as the Gamaliels are referred to other social welfare agencies, such as Sephardic *Bikur Holim* in Brooklyn.

Jeanette Cattan is the worker at *Bikur Holim* who has been involved with the Gamaliels for the past few years. A Syrian immigrant herself, Mrs. Kaltan knows the difficulties of resettlement. (She holds a degree in chemical engineering, but is not pursuing that career.) With all the good that *Bikur Holim* does (its bulletin speaks of visiting the ill and aged, medical services, clothing, psychological counseling, tutoring, baby-sitting, summer camp, rent, and food stamps), its resources are limited.

When Mrs. Gamaliel pleaded for a three-bedroom apartment amid the neat brick homes and flats from Newkirk Avenue and Avenue H, she was told none was available. Landlords and rental agents in Ocean Parkway, many of whom are Syrian Jews, simply were not receptive to her plight. When several people suggested that *Bikur Holim* buy into one of the many cooperatives in the area (if rent runs $800, how much more would a monthly mortgage held by the agency cost?), the proposal was referred to the agency's board for consideration. There was no action on that proposal, or to another coming from Ohio that offered $10,000 for a down payment on such a flat. Shown an apartment in *Bikur Holim*'s own building, Mrs. Gamaliel was forced to turn it down for several reasons: (1) there was no access via elevator (she literally had to crawl in through a side entrace), (2) there were only two small bedrooms, unacceptable for four children, one of them a growing boy, and (3) there was no room to maneuver a wheelchair in the kitchen or bathroom. Orli had to leave her chair downstairs when she entered the building and by mistake, she left her purse, which contained the rent, in cash, for her Williamsburg apartment. When she and Kaltan returned to the chair, the money was gone.[9]

Just before the start of the school year, late in August, 1988, the Gamaliels finally moved into an apartment in Ocean Parkway. The move was accomplished through the combined efforts of Kaltan and the professional staff at *Bikur Holim,* aides to Congressman Stephen Solarz, Judy Carr, and the Schermer Trust of Youngstown, Ohio. The current landlord is unhappy about having a cripple in his building and refuses to make any modifications (a ramp at the side entry, temporary widening of the doorway into the bathroom) that might make Orli more comfortable. Mrs. Gamaliel has been described as "skinny as Hell" and "in mortal agony." She faces another set of surgical procedures that may never relieve her physical pain. Now, however, her eyes well with tears of pride as she watches her children marching off to a decent school ("they look like a million dollars," noted a friend) and her husband is learning English through use of a tape recorder ("he's like a man reborn").

It cannot be a storybook ending. But at least the memories of Williamsburg and rats are fading. Gabi was Bar Mitzvahed in Jerusalem in August 1989. And for the first time in more than a decade, there is hope for this tormented family.

6

Freedom to Emigrate

Commenting on the traditional persecution that Jews have encountered under Islamic rule, S. D. Goitein has written, "Those who live in a country which discriminates against them most blatantly want to have at least one right: to leave that country."[1] Article 13 of the Universal Declaration of Human Rights adopted by the United Nations affirms that principle: "Everyone has the right to freedom of movement and residence within the borders of each state. Everyone has the right to leave any country, including his own, and to return to his country." Article 14 of the same charter adds: "Everyone has the right to seek and to enjoy in other countries asylum from persecution."[2]

All nations, to some extent, hedge on these grand-sounding phrases. The Western democracies frown on travel to countries that sponsor international terrorism. The Soviet Union, with a constitution that guarantees every form of liberty, simply is more flagrant in its totalitarian disregard of the right of emigration. Following in the mode of Nazi Germany, the borders of the Soviet Union and its satellites are hermetically sealed—by barbed wire, ditches, land mines, and armed patrols. The only people who get out are the ones the Soviets decide should leave. In like manner, the Syrian government, a signatory to the Universal Declaration of Human Rights, whose constitution speaks repeatedly of freedom and the integrity of the family unit, treats unsanctioned Jewish flight as a crime. Hence, the attack on Mrs. Gamaliel and her family.

How the Assad government will respond to escapes at any given moment is difficult to predict. In the fall of 1971, twelve Jews, the youngest aged four, were detained five months for planning to flee. Two of these, Joseph Swed and

Nissim Katri, actually remained in jail until September, 1974. When he was released, Swed was crippled, lacked all his teeth, and was permanently insane. During the late 1970s, the punishment was reduced to a few weeks in prison. In December, 1986, however, the Syrians decided to deal harshly again with illegal emigrants. When the Buso family, consisting of fourteen people, tried to cross the border into Turkey, they were apprehended and imprisoned for three months. Three members of the family, including the seventy-year-old patriarch who had suffered broken ribs as a result of torture, were tossed into an underground cell with a small air shaft.[3] Their arrests followed the apprehension of another group of refugees who attempted to flee Syria, against all advice, on Rosh Hashanah in September, 1986. Easily identified by the light of a full moon, this second group (led by Rabbi Leon Guindi, thirty-five, a Hebrew-school teacher; Toufik Khaffif, sixty, a dry goods salesman; and his son Divo, eighteen) compounded their error by carrying with them Syrian money. Just as in Nazi Germany, the Syrians had decreed that the smuggling of money was a capital crime.

As of this writing none of these men were still in Syrian prisons. Perhaps the personal intervention of former President Jimmy Carter to Assad when the two men met in Damascus in March led to a general amnesty in April.[4] If anyone doubts the Ba'athist government's willingness to enforce the letter of the law, however, let them consider the following two cases.

Shimon Khabash was the youngest of six children from an impoverished Jewish family in Damascus.[5] His father was a *shammes,* a caretaker. In 1967, when the boy was barely ten years old, he fainted and turned blue. The boy was seen by a Jewish physician in a clinic (at the time Jewish doctors were denied hospital privileges, a condition since rectified by the Assad regime), and Shimon's family sought permission to travel to Lebanon or France for medical treatment. Twice the request was submitted to the *Muhabarat,* and both times it was rejected. Even after two other doctors, one French and the other Czech, urged that Shimon be sent to Beirut for more specialized care, the government demurred because the boy was Jewish. In those days, not only were Jews refused permission to leave Syria, they were not supposed to travel more than 3 kilometers from their homes. The Jewish ghettos of Damascus, Aleppo, and Al-Qāmishlī were detention centers.

As Shimon once said, "I had no medical treatment from 1967 to 1973." His condition deteriorated until Dr. Ronald Feld in Canada attempted to intercede. "I heard it on the radio," said Shimon. "He's a Canadian doctor. He cares. Because of this radio report of a doctor in Canada who wished to help me, my brothers and sisters were able to persuade my parents that I, the youngest of six and sickly, must escape from Damascus. A Jew on the outside cared about me! I would get help.

"After this news in 1972 that a Canadian doctor wanted to help, my brother was encouraged to go to the Minister of Interior in Damascus for a visa. Suddenly,

Shimon Khabash, 1974. Photo courtesy of the National Task Force for Syrian Jews of the Canadian Jewish Congress.

yes, I could go to Lebanon. But moments before I was to leave came the notice: 'Permission denied; you are a Jew.'

"At the end of 1972, in desperation my brother posed as a Lebanese and obtained two traveling permits. We were discovered and sent back to Damascus by the Syrian secret police. In early 1973, my brother gave five hundred dollars (collected by our poor Jewish community) to a Syrian Arab to smuggle me to Lebanon. At the border he turned me over to the police. My five brothers and sisters were arrested and beaten. Six months later, in June, 1973, a one-month visa was granted after the Syrian police were paid four hundred dollars. My parents were imprisoned. Regardless of this payment, I think someone must have said something for me! There must have been a reason they let me go."

Arriving in Beirut, sick, without money, Shimon found the synagogue and introduced himself to the rabbi. The Beirut community, itself menaced by Palestinian *fedayeen* (commandos), supplied medical care for four months, first in a small hospital (Mar Alias), then at the American University, and finally in a convalescent hospital. When Syrian authorities demanded Shimon's return, his doctors objected, stating further medical treatment was required in Europe. $1,200 more was paid to the *Muhabarat* for a passport. None was ever sent.

Shimon Khabash did flee Lebanon, again illegally, with a group of Syrian escapees bound for France. Supported by the Feld Foundation, he was placed with an Egyptian-Jewish family in Israel in 1973. Described by one visitor as "tall, slim, blond, handsome . . . a bluish tinge around his lips the only sign of his illness,"[6] he was just beginning to learn Hebrew. Doctors in Israel were confident they could help the boy, but wished they had been able to operate on his heart earlier. On February 12, 1975, as I was preparing to travel to Toronto to give a lecture on the status of Jews in Arab lands, my wife received a long-distance phone call from Mrs. Judy Feld. Shimon Khabash had undergone surgery that day at Tel Hashomer hospital in Tel Aviv. He died on the operating table. He was just eighteen years old. He had been denied medical attention, not because he was a Zionist or a warrior, but simply because he was a Jew.

People who have heard this tale often ask what happened to the Khabash family, which was under house arrest. After a period of some months, the restrictions were relaxed. Years later, the Assad government visited another torment on the family. In 1982, one of Shimon's brothers developed a brain tumor. As before, the family implored permission to send the young man out of the country for surgery. This time, no amount of pleading or money moved the *Muhabarat*. The brother died in Syria.[7]

The second incident was made public by the *New York Times* on April 14, 1974. Reporting from Paris, Henry Kamm told of an extraordinary demonstration that had taken place in Damascus that week. Nearly 1,000 Jews from that city's ghetto had taken to the streets to protest the brutal murder of six young people who had attempted to escape from Syria. According to Kamm, the Jewish marchers were joined by an equal number of Arab men and women who shouted condemnations of government harassment of their Jewish neighbors.[8]

In fact, this singular show of Arab-Jewish fraternity did occur, but not quite in the way described. Several thousand persons assembled in silence before the entry to the Haret el-Yahud (the Jewish ghetto), then started walking toward the U.S. Embassy, carrying the caskets of the dead. Said one observer, "Everyone was willing to die, if necessary."[9] Police and soldiers did not let the march proceed very far before dousing the demonstrators with red-tinted hot water from fire hoses at a distance of 100 feet. The protest was ended in a matter of minutes. If it was intended to have any impact on the Assad government, the march had failed.

What prompted the demonstration was the murder of Fara Zeibak (twenty-four), her two sisters Lulu (twenty-three) and Mazal (twenty-two), and their cousin Eva Saad (eighteen).[10] On March 2, 1974, the bodies of these four Jewish girls were discovered by border police in a cave at Asfura in the Zabdani Mountains northwest of Damascus. The girls apparently had contracted with a band of smugglers to take them to Lebanon. Instead, they were raped and murdered. One victim had her ring finger ripped off and all of the bodies were so badly burned only one, the fattest, could be positively identified. Nearby, police found the remains of two Jewish boys, Natan Shaya (eighteen) and Kassam Abadi (twenty), victims of an earlier massacre, their bodies also mutilated. In the most

Clockwise from top left: Fara Zeibak, Mazal Zeibak, Eva Saad, and Lulu Zeibak. While trying to flee from Damascus Ghetto in February 1978, the four women were raped, murdered, and mutilated. Photos courtesy of the National Task Force for Syrian Jews of the Canadian Jewish Congress.

grotesque of gestures, Syrian authorities deposited the bodies of all six in sacks before the homes of their parents in the Jewish ghetto of Damascus. (Another report indicates that the bodies were discovered at dawn in a street in the Jewish quarter.)[11]

Concerned that the killings might appear to be linked with government policy, the Syrians issued a statement disclaiming any responsibility for the crime and pressed an investigation. On March 16, Interior Minister Ali Zaza announced that state security forces had apprehended the culprits. "The four young women were killed," he declared, "by a gang of murderers and smugglers consisting of two Syrian citizens of the Jewish faith and two Muslims who have already been arrested and will be prosecuted."[12]

Syrian-Jewish emigrés around the world were stunned to learn that the accused included Yussef Shalouh, a prominent textile trader, and Azur Zalta, a school teacher. Both men were regarded as outstanding members of the Jewish community. As one communiqúe issued by the Committee of Concern (a nonsectarian U.S. group headed by General Lucius Clay, Bayard Rustin, Archibald MacLeish, Hubert Humphrey, Louis Auchincloss, and Helen Hayes) noted:

People who know the young men well say they are known for their devotion to the welfare of their harassed brethren. For example, both Shaluh and Zalta regularly visited Jewish prisoners and brought them food. Shaluh, the alleged ringleader of this murderous band, had also intervened on various occasions with the Muhabarat on behalf of Jewish prisoners. It is thus highly inconceivable that these devoted members of the Jewish community would murder four of their fellow Jews.[13]

What made the charges even more incredible was the fact that Shalouh was the brother-in-law of Eva Saad. Still, Syrian officials, claiming they had confessions from the prisoners, proceeded with a preliminary indictment in the spring. That the two men may have confessed to contacting the smugglers is not surprising. Jewish merchants in Damascus had been sending nylon fabrics into Lebanon, where they were in short supply, for some time. As activists interested in helping their people leave Syria, Shalouh and Zalta were almost expected to be the contact men with smugglers. Finally, considering the nature of Syrian prisons and the standard of torture used in examinations, confessions should not have surprised anyone. Although the two Muslims accused of the crime, Izzedin and Leila, were given attorneys and subjected to psychiatric examinations, Shalouh and Zalta wallowed in solitary confinement. Their only visitor for some weeks was an American, Jonathan Bates, who found them depressed, when he dropped off food parcels and personal items.[14]

As the date approached for the formal opening of proceedings (June 19, 1974) in the State Security Court, protests mounted against what Israeli Justice Haim Cohn called "a judicial murder and a vile blood libel." In France, the journals *Figaro* and *Combat* inquired rhetorically whether the Syrian government intended to conduct an anti-Semitic show trial in Damascus. In Italy, *La Voce Republicana* expressed concern over potential massive pogroms, and its sister journal *Epoca* dispatched a correspondent to Damascus who reported that the Syrian press was conducting a hate campaign so vicious that "killing a Jew looks like a virtue." The same correspondent, Livio Caputo, asked two other prominent Damascus Jews (Selim Totah and Joseph Jejati) in the presence of *Muhabarat* observers why the girls would have wanted to run away. Their answer was that "they were poor, uneducated girls, textile workers. The old father of the Zebah (*sic*) girls is an untutored man, and the mother is very sick. Maybe somebody deceived them, telling that they could find a better life elsewhere. Maybe they were afraid that they could not get married, for there are few young men in our community. One day they disappeared leaving a note on the sewing machine saying that Azur Zalta, one of our teachers, knew about their departure. When no further tidings came from them, their parents confronted Azur and informed the government, and the terrible truth came to light."[15]

In Canada, Foreign Minister Mitchell Sharp promised to make diplomatic soundings through the Canadian Embassy in Beirut and Amnesty International. From New York, the Committee of Concern offered, "In view of the suspicious circumstances surrounding this incident and past evidence of 'confessions' extracted under torture, we call upon the Syrian authorities to assure that the alleged criminals be furnished with defense counsel of their choosing and given a prompt and open trial." The U.S. National District Attorneys' Association volunteered to supply counsel for the defendants or, failing that, to attend the trial as representatives of the world community.

The Syrian government reacted predictably. Minister Zaza fulminated against what he termed "the orchestrated press campaign that has been going on abroad about the case." Under secretary for Foreign Affairs al-Rifai added, "Any negotiation on the circumstances of Syrian citizens of the Jewish faith would be an unlawful interference in the internal affairs of our country. The problems that concern them come entirely under our jurisdiction."[16]

For a time, at least, one democracy concurred with this refrain so reminiscent of veiled warnings issued by Nazi Germany in the 1930s. Beset with correspondence urging intervention on behalf of Shalouh and Zalta, the U.S. State Department had responded that the plight of the Jewish community in Syria was "an internal Syrian problem." Embarrassed by the outcry these words had elicited, the Nixon administration backed off somewhat. On May 13, State Department spokesman Paul J. Hare explained that the government was "concerned about the fate of the Jewish community in Syria," but that the department felt "the best way to assist them was through diplomatic channels."[17] Nixon was obviously hedging his bets for an upcoming visit to Syria in June of that year. He would be the first incumbent U.S. president to visit Damascus and in the midst of torrents of criticism associated with the Watergate scandal, the president, who was smitten with his self-image as an innovator in foreign affairs, did not want to jeopardize that prestigious moment.[18]

World opinion did force some modification of Syrian lynch law. Before the trial resumed in August, charges against the two Jews were changed. Now Shalouh and Zalta were accused of giving assistance in "an illegal escape from Syria to an enemy country." At that, the world was left to ponder how Lebanon, the destination of the six murdered Jewish youths, could be labeled "an enemy country" or whether such "illegal flight" would have been undertaken if Syria adhered to basic standards of civilized law. Such questions became moot in September, 1974, when after being incarcerated for several months and having their trial "continued," both Shalouh and Zalta were released on bail. While speaking with the brother of one of the men, the trial judge let it be known that the accused should be told, "Bye-bye." The government had no further use for judicial proceedings and wanted the matter closed.[19]

It is not that simple. Since 1975, special prayer services have been held annually all over the world as memorials to the four slain Jewish girls. In Canada, Sweden, Brazil, India, Italy, South Africa, Denmark, Israel, France, and the United States, rabbis have dedicated Shabbat Zachor, which falls in February or March, as a Sabbath of remembrance and action for the Jews of Syria. Officials such as former New York Governor Hugh Carey and Mayor Edward Koch have joined these protests by issuing proclamations. And poetry has been written about the four.

> My four sisters
> The blood that flowed from you
> Was my blood too,
> The misuse of you
> The dismembered members
> Were mine too.
>
> I heard him grin at Damascus Gate,
> From this one I shall break
> A breast,
> From this her shapely leg
> And small white ear,
> From that a Jewish arm
> And a cleft,
> And from this one,
> She is so pretty—
> Just a tongue.
>
> If you see my Syrian sisters weeping in Damascus Ghetto,
> Tell them
> Their daughters' tongues
> Have been grafted onto mine.[20]

To this day, no one has ever been punished for the rape-murders of the three Zeibak sisters and Eva Saad. Azur Zalta eventually managed to leave Syria for the United States. When I arranged to meet and talk with him in Brooklyn in September, 1986, he failed to show. A frightened man, old before his time, he contemplates returning to Damascus.

7

The Bahats

There is no higher duty in Judaism than the preservation of human life. The Talmud enjoins "the greatest in Israel" to act himself and promptly when another being is in peril (Tosephta Shabbat 16). Rescue efforts may not violate rules against idolatry, immorality, or the shedding of innocent life (Ber. 61b, Mish. Yoma 8:7, Ket. 19a). Nor should such actions be so reckless (e.g., racing into a ruined building) that they jeopardize the rescuer. According to Shabbat 32a, "A man should never court danger in the hope that he will be miraculously delivered."

In every age, individual Jews have had to balance obligations to their fellow men and to themselves. In practice, *mesirat nephesh* (self-sacrifice) often has superseded concern for *pikuach nephesh* (rescuing life). The tradition of Jewish martyrdom goes back to the age of the Maccabees when the priest Eleazer along with Hannah and her seven sons refused to abjure their faith. Thousands of *Kiddush ha-Shem* were burned to death by self-possessed Rhenish crusaders and Dominican inquisitors. But the greatest test was demanded during the Holocaust.

When German Jews underwent their first legal persecutions at the hands of the Nazis in 1933, Rabbi Leo Baeck, a leader of the Berlin community, advised his kinsmen to "wear the Yellow Star with pride." During the war years, when other European leaders, knowing their lives were in danger, fled their occupied homelands, Rabbi Baeck elected to stay with his people, counseling them through deportations to the transit ghetto of Terezin and then to Auschwitz. Amazingly, the seventy-two-year-old Baeck survived the Holocaust, one of the few aged rabbis who did.[1]

In 1943, the last three rabbis in the Warsaw ghetto faced an identical dilemma. When Catholic prelates proposed to hide rabbis Menahem Zemba, Samson Stockhamer, and David Shapiro, Shapiro, who was the youngest, declared, "We already know that we cannot help our people, but by staying with them, and by not abandoning them, we encourage them and strengthen their hopes, and this is the only encouragement we are able to give the last Jews. I simply do not have the strength to abandon these wretched people." Although the decision would cost them their lives, all three elected to stay.[2]

Each of these men responded to tyranny in a similar noble fashion. Although acdemics may debate Rabbi Beck's alleged arrogance for not telling his countrymen of mobile gas vans in 1941, of gas chambers two years later, or of the senselessness of the Warsaw rabbis' sacrifice, the ordeal of spiritual leaders continues—in the Soviet Union and Syria. When should an individual put aside his responsibilities to family or community and seek personal refuge? Does a rabbi, fearing for his personal safety or that of his own family, have the right to abandon his community?

Those very questions were recently posed by a Syrian rabbi. A gaunt, elderly man with wisps of a beard, Rabbi Yehudah asked, "Should rabbis come first or last?" Then without waiting for a response, he pointed out that in Israel, unlike the Arab states, the captain goes first, in short, he serves as the point for his men. In like manner, if a vessel sinks, the captain remains behind until the very last. Historically, rabbis have been the first to absorb shocks for their people, the last to abandon them. "Where is it written," asked the rabbi, "that after forty years of service, I should sacrifice my life as well?"[3]

People who live in the comfort of the free world may have opinions as to the propriety of flight, but none of them may judge the actions of the Syrian rabbis. Eliahu Bahat was a rabbi who stayed. The eldest of eight Jewish children raised in Aleppo, Bahat remained in Syria when the rest of his family (including an aged mother) emigrated in 1947. The 17,000 Jews who lived in Aleppo until the end of World War II constituted the backbone of that city's middle class. They were bankers, journalists, commercial agents, and craftsmen. The town counted ten synagogues, including the ancient Bashita synagogue, which was considered among the most beautiful in the Middle East. According to Moishe Cohen of the world Organization of Jews from Arab countries (WOJAC), "Many of the Jews of Aleppo came from Spain, Italy, Turkey. Many of them had passports and identity cards from France, Britain, Iraq. In Aleppo, the Jews lived in two quarters—the Jamiliyeh, which in Arabic means 'beautiful,' a very beautiful quarter, because they were rich—and the other part of the community lived in the Hartal Yahud (Jewish quarter). All those who lived in the Jewish quarter of Aleppo either left Syria or moved to the other quarter."[4]

For the most part, Aleppo's Jews were quiescent and non-Zionist. In 1936, they cabled their support for the Syrian independence delegation in Paris and, during the war years, avoided rousing suspicions of the Vichy French and their protofascist allies in occupied Syria.

With the defeat of the Nazis, Arab nationalist sentiments were fueled. A return to British or French colonialism and the creation of a Jewish state in the Middle East were deemed intolerable. As early as the end of March, 1945, Arab students rioted in Damascus as an expression of their opposition to Zionism. Heeding the cry of Muslim leaders to jihad, on November 2, 1945, mobs ravaged Jewish communities in Cairo, Alexandria, Port Said, and Al-Mansūrah in Egypt; and Zanzur, Tripoli, Az-Zāwiyah, Cussabat, and Zilten in Libya. Eventually, the pogrom mentality affected Aleppo. On November 18, 1945, a group of Arabs vandalized the great synagogue, smashed memorial candles burning before the *Aron Kodesh*, beat two old Jews, and burned prayer books in the streets.

For the next three years, the Syrian government operated in a schizophrenic fashion toward its Jewish population—brutalizing them, yet trying to frustrate efforts at emigration. Technically, the borders to Palestine were sealed and Syrian Arabs who were absentee landlords were discouraged from transferring their holdings in Palestine to Jews. Syria's Jews faced discrimination in jobs, education, and taxes. They were also slaughtered in riots that were orchestrated by the government. Two days after the United Nations voted to partition Palestine, the Jews of Aleppo were subjected to their own *Kristallnacht*. On December 1, 1947, every synagogue in the city, five schools, one orphanage, a youth club, 150 homes, and fifty shops were destroyed. More than one hundred Torahs were desecrated, including an ancient Masoretic text, while police and firemen watched. Five months later, on April 28, 1948, several Aleppo rabbis appealed to their American counterparts, "The Arab mobs are raging and threatening our lives. Hurry up, help us! The water is engulfing us."[5]

Before the state of Israel was proclaimed, most of Syria's Jews managed to escape. From an estimated 40,000, their number shrank to 4,000, most of whom remained in Damascus. About 1,000 were left in Aleppo to respond to the sneering questions of their Western kinsmen who wondered why any had stayed behind.[6] There were legitimate reasons, of course, many of them reminiscent of the thought processes that dictated actions of German Jews who "should have recognized" the warning signs of genocide in the 1930s.[7] Some Syrian Jews were old, too old they believed, to start anew in a different land. Some were proud of their roots in Syria, which stretched back generations and could be read on the tombstones in Jewish cemeteries that would soon be razed for road construction. Others were too poor or afraid of the physical hazards posed by relocation. A few were kept behind as hostages, guarantors of good behavior (e.g., non-Zionist activity) of their families.

When his family departed from Aleppo in 1947, Rabbi Bahat volunteered to stay behind as the vouchsafe. He had another motive for staying, however, and that was his belief that the Jewish remnant would need a spiritual leader as well as *shohet* (kosher butcher). Rabbi Bahat was confronted with the very dilemma posed by Rabbi Yehudah—to flee or risk martyrdom; others had run. Rabbi Ibrahim Hamra of Damascus, meanwhile, has remained with his people, although many, knowing too well the capricious nature of Syrian justice, have implored him to leave.

Bahat was no saint. But in his case, love and courage blended with dedication.

Ruins of Aleppo synagogue. Photo courtesy of the National Task Force for Syrian Jews of the Canadian Jewish Congress.

*Ruins of Aleppo synagogue. Photo courtesy of the National Task Force
for Syrian Jews of the Canadian Jewish Congress.*

He stayed, and for the next thirty years, this frail, thin man experienced sys-
tematic persecution at the hands of the Kuwatli, Atasi, and Assad regimes. The
Muhabarat monitored his religious services. His identity card, which I have
seen, bore the vivid, red marking *Mussawi* (Jew) no less than ten times. His
seven children were harassed daily. His daughter Shulamit recalled, "Life with
the Arabs was very difficult, difficult for the children to walk, to go by foot.
They fought with the children on the street on the way to school. In school,
everything was *asur* [forbidden]. The manager was an Arab. *Asur* on Israel,
asur al Medinat Yisrael [forbidden to talk about the state of Israel], *asur* on
Zionism. There was a curfew after 8:00 P.M. You couldn't go from your house.
It was *kashe m'od* [very hard] for Jews in Syria. Even if you went to the
university, it was very hard. There was no work for Jews."[8]

"*Ayn atid*. There was no future. You lived your life in fear, all the time. It
was no life. You never knew when you answered the door if you might be shot.
The Syrians are *meshugayyim* [crazy people]." The voice was that of a brother,
Simcha, a robust man in his thirties. "Our father was at the *mishtara* [police]
all the time. During the Six Day War, they cleared the streets, gathered all the
Jews in their houses for about a week. During the Yom Kippur War, my father
was stabbed with a knife, in his own shop."[9]

In March, 1973, Simcha Bahat decided to run away. "I was sixteen years old, the first from the family to escape, to Beirut, over the mountains. There were two families, about thirty people altogether. There were many problems crossing the border. We went three days *baderech* [by foot]. At the Syrian border, the guards asked us where we were going. I was dressed like an Arab. Exactly three days before was a Muslim holiday. The police grabbed me because I had a false passport—an Arab identity card. They said if I had money I could go to Lebanon. Otherwise, I would have to stay in Syria. I had a little money. I was afraid to stay in Syria. I had two Muslim friends who helped me. They gave me perhaps $1,000. Why? They were friends of mine. Later, I paid them back after I got work."

Following Simcha's escape, a brother and two sisters fled Syria. On each occasion, Rabbi Bahat was arrested, taken to prison and tortured for one month. "I just left in the morning from school," says Simcha Bahat. "*Halachti v'bar-achti* [I went and I escaped]. But they arrested my mother and father and said they should have known where I was going." According to Rabbi Bahat's children, he was bastinadoed (beaten on the feet), given electric shocks on his body and arms, dumped into a filthy cell where water dripped from the walls. Dripping blood, he was denied access to a latrine. The beatings left Eliahu Bahat weak and with kidney failure.

By 1979, his health had deteriorated to such a point (the rabbi also had contracted bladder cancer) that relatives living outside Syria feared he might soon die. Bahat's Syrian doctors ("no good," insist the children) conceded there wasn't much they could do for him. A sister living in Canada raised $1,000 ("I think it went to the *Muhabarat*," says Shulamit) and an exit permit was secured. Even then, the Syrians tried to confound the rabbi's departure.

The rabbi was supposed to arrive in Toronto via KLM on a *Wednesday,* when his Canadian immigration papers would be ready. Friends had also arranged for kosher food in transit and for an ambulance to be at the airport that day. On *Monday* morning, Rabbi Bahat's relatives were notified he was coming in that same day—via Lufthansa. The pilot of the German plane had radioed ahead that the rabbi was in critical condition. Bahat declined to eat anything, save one banana, which he had brought with him. Moreover, he was bleeding internally and was on a catheter.

At this point, the rabbi's relatives secured the assistance of Judy Feld, then president of Beth Tzedec, Toronto's largest synagogue. With some difficulty, Mrs. Feld badgered government bureaucrats to expedite the necessary entry permit on an emergency basis. She also arranged to have doctors from Mt. Sinai Hospital on the spot when the plane landed. As the rabbi was taken by stretcher to the ambulance, he kissed the hands of those who went with him, sobbing, "Merci, merci." Physicians who treated the emaciated, broken man observed they had not seen anything like him since they liberated the Nazi death camps. "They [the Syrians] tore him to pieces," said one doctor.[10]

Two more daughters, Shulamit and Chave, subsequently made their way to freedom after substantial bribes and diplomatic interventions. Shulamit, a vivacious brunette, came out in 1980. At the time, Canada's relations with the Assad government were strained; the closest Canadian ambassador was in Beirut. The problem was that Shulamit, who sought an exit permit to take care of her ailing father, could not travel from Syria to Lebanon to pick up her Canadian entry permit. When the British Embassy in Damascus was asked to perform this service, it declined, feigning concern over security and terrorism (!) and saying it was not customary to issue Canadian papers for Jews. To which a minister in Ottawa fumed, "What is this? World War II?"[11]

As the deadline for Shulamit's departure drew near, other possibilities were discussed (perhaps issuing a visa through the German or Australian embassy in Damascus). Finally, on January 12, 1980, the Canadian ambassador drove to the Syrian capital, registered at the Medran Hotel, and notified a member of the family to come physically from Aleppo to pick up the visa that led to Shulamit's freedom.

Chave's passage to freedom was even more convoluted. Twenty-one years old, she pressed the *Muhabarat* with a story that a *shiddoch* (arranged marriage) had been set for her by Syrian Jews in the United States. For eleven months, the family negotiated with the state police. An initial payment of $3,000 resulted in the issuance of exit permits valid only for Turkey. Several weeks and several thousand dollars later, the government granted her papers for Canada. There would be a third shakedown before she left on January 23, 1983, bringing the cost of her liberty to $16,000.

When Chave arrived in Toronto, immigration authorities proved shockingly insensitive. As the jumbo KLM jet landed one Sunday, relatives and friends waited at the glass partition near customs. When the girl did not appear, Chave's uncle went to investigate and discovered that "a runt of an immigration officer" had plucked Chave out of line. Huskier, swarthier, and less attractive than her sister Shulamit, unable to speak anything but Arabic, lacking even the entry permit that was to be delivered to her at the airport, Chave apparently fitted the airport's profile of a potential terrorist. Dumped into a large room by herself, she awaited further questioning. When her aunt and uncle arrived, they found the terrified girl clutching a suitcase (filled not with bombs, but presents for the people who had rescued her). When Chave saw her family, she burst into tears. At that, the immigration officer turned to her uncle and asked, "*Atah m'dabare Ivrit?* [Do you speak Hebrew?]" It happened that this bureaucrat who was scrupulously following instructions was a Jew himself.[12]

Today, Shulamit Bahat lives in a neat little apartment in a rennovated section of Jaffa with her two infant children and husband. Her sister Chave is single, living nearby in Holon. Simcha Bahat is a gifted, multilingual technician, the father of a little boy who bears his grandfather's name: Eliahu. Rabbi Bahat's children are unanimous in their praise of the woman who helped their family, Judy Feld—"an angel from *shamayim*." They also fear for their one sister, Devorah, left in Syria with several children.

"She can't leave," says Shulamit, echoing the fear of Jews who had relatives in Germany or Poland. "They don't let the whole family out. They keep one of the family. They know that if the whole family comes out, they won't go back. *Bvadai* [certainly], they are keeping her as a hostage. Like the Americans who were hostages to Khomeini."

"They are prisoners of war," adds Simcha. "It won't be good for Syria if Jews get out. The Syrians want to think, 'Better for Syria for them to be in Syria than Israel.' "[13]

Neither Rabbi Bahat nor his wife were able to enjoy freedom with their children. The rabbi's wife had suffered from heart problems for several years. In 1981, just two days before Rosh Hashanah, the Syrians suddenly let it be known they would permit Mrs. Bahat to emigrate. What they failed to mention to correspondents abroad was that the woman had died one month before. The *Muhabarat* wished to transfer her corpse to Canada—for the sum of $10,000.

Eliahu Bahat knew none of this. The rabbi recovered from his own physical pain long enough to fulfill one last dream. In June, 1979, he had tea with his ninety-seven-year-old mother on a veranda in Israel. Three months later, on the eve of Tishah b'Ab, the anniversary of the destruction of the ancient temples in Jerusalem and the expulsion of his ancestors from Spain, he died. For some time, the rest of his family in Syria did not know. The Orthodox Jewish family was denied the right to sit *shiva* or say *kaddish*, to mourn properly for their father, a man who had chosen *mesirat nephesh*.

8

Purim 1986

Years ago, a millionaire decried efforts of the Youngstown Zionist District to sponsor an organization for Jewish college students from the Middle East. Speaking in a heavy accent, this man, himself an immigrant from Tsarist Russia, declared, "They [Sephardic Jews] don't think like us. They don't act like us. They don't look like us."[1] James R. was reflecting the very bigotry that has frustrated the integration of "Oriental Jews" into Israeli society for forty years. He was, it is hoped, reciting a litany that belongs to the past.

Any notion that there is something different about Syrian Jews, that somehow they are racially inferior, would have been dispelled by watching two of the Bahat children cavort about a table filled with cookies and fruit. Aliza, Shulamit's eighteen-month-old daughter, was a bubbly little princess with a winning smile. Her chubby, blond, blue-eyed cousin, Simcha's son who was just a year old, was equally captivating. Munching on a banana, like any toddler, the boy was something special—a Ninja warrior. Like Jewish children everywhere, the Bahats were costumed to celebrate Purim.

A gay, carnival festival, not unlike Mardi Gras, Purim commemorates the rescue of Jews from massacre at the hands of a fourth-century B.C. Persian tyrant. Traditionally, children donned customs of characters mentioned in the book of Esther (King Ahasuerus, the villain Haman, Queen Ester, and her kinsman Mordecai) and attended religious services, where with noisemakers called *gragers,* they attempted to blot out every mention of Haman's name.

They still use the noisemakers in Israel as well as the loud, infectious Chasidic music that ripples down the hillsides of Ahuza. Normally abstemious adults still throw their inhibitions to the wind and get *shikkered* (drunk) on Purim. Some

Children in an Aleppo synagogue wearing prayer shawls sent from Canada. Photo courtesy of the National Task Force for Syrian Jews of the Canadian Jewish Congress.

of the customs have changed, however. Like the Bahats, children at the Nof Panorama resemble cowboys, punk rockers, Superman, and ballerinas more than characters from the Biblical tale. The change is also evident among adults who have seized on Purim as an excuse to hold masked balls before the onset of more sober holidays such as Passover and Yom ha-Shoah.

So it was that an interview with the Hadli brothers had to be shifted from one Tel Aviv hotel (the Palace) to the lobby of another (the Grand Beach) in March, 1986 because of the many revelers who made discussion nearly impossible. Although it was Purim (to which the Israelis devote three days of merrymaking), no one would have known it by the Hadlis. As they entered the hotel, Nahum (twenty-nine), Moishe (twenty-six), Josef (twenty-five), and Dovid (twenty-four) were no different from Jews in Deal or Shaker Heights in their dark, double-breasted, pin-striped suits. These were their Sabbath clothes and they would not meet with me until after sundown on Saturday. Two of their younger brothers were at home, but I assumed they were much like the four who sat with me—dark, short, and stocky, built like professional football blocking guards. Only the two eldest were fluent in English, which was understandable because Nahum was the person who had fled Syria in 1973 with Rabbi Isaac F. of Deal, N.J.

Nahum began their story. "We were from Aleppo, my mother, father, and ten children. I don't know how long we had lived there, maybe hundreds of years. My father is close to seventy. We worked in gold, silver, metalworkers. We had an apartment, a building with four or five apartments. Every apartment was worth fifty thousand dollars. Nice, big. The total worth was around two hundred and fifty thousand dollars. We couldn't sell it. When we left, the Syrian government got it.

"All the people in Aleppo were religious, really religious, not like the *Mea Shearim*,[2] but the *Mizrachi*.[3] All of them studied Torah half the day and worked the other half. Life was regular. They [the Syrian Arabs] didn't interfere too much. 'Hallo! Hallo!' from afar, but not too much. They did make trouble sometimes. We had fights with them. They cursed the Jews. That was nothing, normal. If somebody fights you, they might take him to the police, but the police wouldn't put him in jail or punish him. Most of the time, they didn't get involved."[4]

A change in the Syrian administrative hierarchy usually meant new regulations, a degrading census, and the roughing up of people in the streets, as new officials tried through severity to impress their superiors. As one refugee testified, "In order to justify his actions, the Commissioner decided to incriminate the Jews and prove publicly their hostility to the regime. He instructed one of the leaders of the community to provide him within a fortnight with all the expressions by Jews against the regime."Nahum Hadli recalled the ongoing harassment. "Sometimes when my father had a little shop, the police would take money. Not too much, just a little money. They would come in and take this and that, little things, soap and things for hair. My father was in jail many times. The first time was in 1956. Once, somebody told the Syrians that he wanted to go to Israel, that he was encouraging people to go to Israel. But he didn't do this. They beat him for two weeks. When I escaped, they put him in jail. Then again in 1978, when they tried to get out.[5]

"I came out fourteen years ago, when I was fifteen. The three [Zeibak] girls were killed about the same time. I didn't ask my mother and father. I just ran away from home. Because every person who is there wants to be in *Eretz Yisroel* because they are Jewish. Not in *Medinat Yisroel,* not in the state of Israel which is not religious. Many rules are against the Torah. But in Syria, every Jewish child wants to go because of the pressure. They press you. They don't want to give anybody anything. Only Jews cannot go out. Only Jews have marked identity cards. Sometimes they marked Christian cards, but not with a red stamp like this—*Mussawi*. And they point—*'Yahud!'* Everybody knows that's Jewish, but not all of them know *Mussawi*. The security police know. Jews in Syria could not make import-exports. In school, they taught nothing about Israel. Only that Israel was the enemy, not a legitimate state. They say it is an Arab country, Palestine, and we have to take the land back.''

Nahum Hadli was more laconic about his escape than his rabbi friend. He made no mention of stolen identity cards or the submarine that whisked them away from Lebanon one night. No mention either of the danger of being kidnapped back to Syria like Isaac Gaddeh and Albert Hasbani, two teenagers, who, like Albert Elia, disappeared off the streets of Beirut.[6]

''You get through the border of Lebanon, before there was fighting. It was nice. Just two people, me and another friend, the same age. We went by car to the border. It wasn't so dangerous because lots of people went out this way. Arabs. They didn't check our passports. No passports, only an identification card. They didn't ask for that. Lots of people crossed to Lebanon and lots didn't have a card. They don't ask if you have a card. There is security, but we went around the Syrian police and went to the Lebanese police. They didn't ask for any passport. They didn't check everybody. The taxi driver who took us to Beirut never asked. The whole thing didn't cost a lot of money—around fifty dollars.

''We went to the Beirut community. I think we saw Albert Elia, but nobody heard of him again. We went to a synagogue and people took care of us for eight months. Then we got to France, and after a couple of days in France we came to Israel. We have relatives here who helped us. I finished school and went into the army.''

Nahum dismissed his escape in a matter-of-fact way, but other refugees have compared flight to the day of judgment ''as if a man did flee from a lion, and a bear met him and went into the house and leaned his hand on the wall, and a serpent bit him'' (Amos 5:19).[7] Nahum's brother Moishe also had a different perception of how easily everything had gone. ''Sometimes the police count the people in the houses. Every one or two years they make a census. They sit in the shul and all the people have to sign up. Everyone has their picture taken, everyone over thirteen. Sometimes they come every day into the homes if they suspect people of trying to leave. Sometimes they're watching them two or three years.

''When [Nahum] left and they arrested our father, we were afraid. I don't remember exactly. They came to our house in regular suits, identified themselves as *Muhabarat* and took him away. But three weeks later and he was back. All three of us [pointing to his younger brothers] were in jail. We were eighteen, sixteen, and fifteen years old. It wasn't easy to get out. We tried to get to Turkey, not Lebanon, and were caught at the border. Near Iskenderun (Alexandretta). By a river ford. The entire family, all eight.''

Nahum added, ''They were caught because every time they tried to leave somebody told the police. Arab people who knew smugglers. If the smugglers weren't good, every time somebody wanted to go they told the police. They paid the smugglers fifteen thousand Syrian liras (four thousand dollars) in 1978 and were betrayed. The entire family was put in jail for two months, including the youngest who was nine years old.''

Moishe continued, "At first we were in an underground prison in Aleppo, small rooms, two to a room. Then in another prison in Damascus that wasn't so big. Most were political prisoners, not criminals. I saw Maurice Nuseyri in jail.[8] He tried to escape to Lebanon and they caught him. He may have had a false passport to Jordan. Perhaps he wanted out because it's not a free country. We were in the same jail for about one week. He was unhappy because he lost a lot of money. The government took the money to let him out, then arrested him. The government sends smugglers to tell the people, 'You want to go out?' and most of the time they then take them to jail.''

Nahum said, "All the time we wrote letters through Canada. There was no direct post to Syria. The secret police opened all the letters. Once, for an entire year, they threw away all the letters. I had nothing to do with their getting out. I was in Israel after visiting New York for a short time. Then three years ago, I got a telephone call from America. Somebody had connections with Turkey, a contact. They left through the border with smugglers, but they were good smugglers.''

Moishe interjected, "Some people in ten families from Damascus got here, but their relatives were put in jail, maybe one or two months.''

Nahum described their life today. "We have a factory now. Most of the family works in Tel Aviv making jewelry. It's hard over here. It's very hard to live a Jewish life. It's very hard work. Taxes. Everything is taxes. In Syria it's very simple to work. No taxes. It's different. In Syria they are more afraid to kill Jews than they are here. Something is not right. There—one, two, three, they punish. Here, you have to be more afraid of the Arabs. Not bombs. You cannot go in the streets of the Old City of Jerusalem if you are Jewish. Two weeks ago they killed one person from Syria. My friend from my class. In his shop. Two Arabs came in and killed him with a knife. They don't publish anything about that. But if somebody does anything against Arabs, they publish that.''

The brothers were unwilling to reveal more than this cursory, almost sanguine tale of existence in Syria to a stranger over tea. A close friend of the family, however, on listening to a tape of our conversations declared, "Their story was not quite the way it happened. The escape is too glib. They went through hell in that prison. That's how Moishe became an epileptic and Dovid a depressive.''[9]

Purim 1986 was a bittersweet experience for me. As the four young men who could have been my students parted, Nahum Hadli expressed what seems to be accepted prophecy among Syrian Jews. "Hafez al-Assad has a lot of enemies. Maybe 85 percent of the people [in Syria] are against him. When he goes, Syria will be like Lebanon. It may be bad for the Jews. It would be better for everyone to get out of Syria before. Maybe if we try hard to work on this, they will. If the American government asks the Syrians, really serious, they will let them out. Assad doesn't care too much about them now.''

9

Abu Wujjah, Father of Pain

Every oppressed people can recite tales of atrocity inflicted on them by an enemy. Palestinians often invoke the destruction of 385 towns by the Zionists and massacres inflicted at Deir Yassin, Qfar Qassim, Qalqīlyah, Sabra, and Shatilla.[1] Western newspapers seem transfixed by reports of Arab students killed in demonstrations at Bir Zeit University and family homes burned by the authorities, of West Bank mayors maimed by car bombings, and children abused in Israeli prisons.[2] When Meir Kahane speaks of ridding *Eretz Yisroel* of Arabs, his words have more than a rhetorical ring for the objects of his hatred.

For some Israelis, the above acts may represent retribution for what happened at Ramat Rahel and Yad Mordechai in 1948, at Kiryat Shimona and Maalot in 1975, at Damour in 1976, along the beaches of Tel Aviv in 1978, and in the alleys of Hebron in 1984. Pain has been repaid for pain and this has been especially true in the case of Syrian-Jewish relations. While it is one thing to fight an enemy, it is quite another to mutilate them. During the Yom Kippur War of 1973, Israel registered a protest with the International Red Cross, detailing forty-two cases where Syrian troops had violated the Geneva Convention of August 12, 1949, regarding treatment of prisoners of war. Specifically:

1. At Nafah on the Golan Heights, an Israeli soldier was found, shot dead while his hands were tied behind his back with telephone wire and bootlaces.

2. At another IDF (Israel Defense Forces) strongpoint on Mt. Hermon, five Israeli prisoners were stripped (a common practice), tortured with rifle butts, then shot while their hands were tied behind their backs with telephone wire. The faces of all five had been shattered with bullets fired at their heads from close range.

3. At Majdal Shams another Israeli soldier was found dead, his shirt and trousers un-buttoned, boots and socks scattered some distance away.

4. At Khushaneya junction, the eyes of a murdered Israeli soldier had been gouged. In fact, the government of Israel submitted information indicating that a Moroccan soldier serving with the Syrian forces had a sack filled with parts of bodies of Israel soldiers (palms and tongues) that he intended to send home as souvenirs.

5. At another forward base, a dead Israeli soldier was found bound in his own phylacteries and stuffed into the desecrated *Aron Kodesh* (ark) of the base.

6. At Dumeir in Syrian territory, an Israeli pilot who parachuted was stabbed to death by Iraqi soldiers who took part in fighting.

7. Six other Israeli pilots were murdered by small-arms fire after they bailed out of their small planes.

8. Israeli POWs were taken by truck to the townlet of Qatanā where Syrian civilians were permitted to pummel the prisoners.

9. Other Syrian prisoners testified that in one instance, Syrian soldiers trampled on the heads of six Israeli soldiers, who represented the crews of two tanks that had been hit.[3]

All of these acts took place, of course, during wartime. Such things are not supposed to happen in Syria where U.N. Ambassador Kelani once asserted, "Jews live as brothers to Syrian Christians and Syrian Muslims. They have equal rights just like other citizens." Repeatedly, however, individual Jews or families have been subjected to physical assault or murder. After the Six Day War, an old man in Damascus was arrested when police saw the flickering flame of his Sabbath oil lamp through the window. They beat him to death, claiming the light was a coded signal to Israelis on the Golan Heights. In the summer of 1971, a Jewish girl in Damascus was arrested, raped by her captors, burned with cigarette butts, and dumped naked into the streets of the ghetto. The *New York Times* reported a case in the first week of January, 1972 where a young man was decapitated in the ghetto and another case where a father was forced to have relations with his own daughter at gunpoint.[4] In 1973, a child was molested in the ghetto and thrown to the ground; she was left with impairments in speech, hearing, and eyesight. In a scene reminiscent of the Abadi murders, Syrian police invaded the home of a Jewish goldsmith in the spring of 1981 to check on whether he was giving aid to the mutinous Muslim Brotherhood. While the husband was detained elsewhere, a guard raped the wife.[5]

For Syrian Jews unfortunate enough to be arrested, detention is not as innoc-uous as recounted by the Hadli brothers (Chapter 8). Locked into cells too small for a standing adult, they lack air or light. The only sanitary facilities are the food vessels that double as chamber pots. Whipping is a daily occurrence and may take the form of the primitive bastinado (as in the case of Rabbi Bahat) or simply bashing a man's head against a wall until he loses his senses. In the summer of 1974, eleven Jewish women from Aleppo were caught as they at-tempted to flee the country and were tortured in a Damascus jail. An escapee told of one woman who "was tied hand and foot with wire, strapped inside a big lorry tire with her head downwards; electric shocks were applied, every five or ten minutes. Gradually the intervals increased, but so did the charge. After thirty-six hours, the woman confessed and was permitted to return home. She awakes shrieking in the night."[6]

Syria's constitution prohibits torture. Yet in its official 1985 report, Amnesty International accused the Assad government of "systematically" violating human rights and detailed thirty-five different kinds of brutality. Among them: (1) the "black slave," which involved strapping a prisoner onto a device that, when switched on, inserts a heated metal skewer into the anus, (2) the "washing machine," a hollow spinning drum in which a victim's arms are spun until they are crushed, and (3) the "Syrian, or confession, chair," a metal seat designed to arch the victim's spine while metal blades fixed to the front legs cut into his ankles. Said Amnesty International, "People tortured on the Syrian chair are said to have suffered fractured vertebrae and near strangulation.[7]

We have already mentioned Joseph Swed who spent three years in Syrian jails. When he was released in September, 1974, Swed was crippled, lacking all his teeth, and permanently insane. Yitzhak Tsur is someone who can empathize with Swed. Tsur, a stocky jeweler from Aleppo, was imprisoned three times by the Syrians. The wonder is that this man whose ancestors came from Spain retained a sense of stability after what he had experienced. (He subsequently fled to Venezuela where he perfected his Spanish.) As we sat on a bench in the Mamilla Park in Jerusalem, it was evident that Syria's prisons had left psychological as well as physical scars on this chain-smoking man.[8] Tsur began:

"I was born in Aleppo in 1943, but on my identity card here, they said '37. It was a kind of mistake and they didn't correct it. I didn't make any issue of it because this way I'll get my pension early. My father and grandfather went hundreds of years back. I don't know the original time when they arrived in Syria. There were about thirty or forty people in the entire family, a large family, all from Aleppo. I had two sisters. I still have family in Syria, my wife's family, too.

"My father was a merchant with a small shop, selling cloth. I studied Jewish education to Talmud, Torah, and yeshiva, secondary education. In 1950, around *Pesach*, my father was arrested. He was smuggling Jews to Israel. From the moment the state of Israel arose, he smuggled people over the mountains to Lebanon. He was the first father arrested for that. He was sentenced to three years in prison, but after one year he was let go. It was the Zaim government. When Zaim was murdered, he was still in prison. So he had both Zaim and Kuwatli.[9]

"They didn't do anything to me. I was only a child, the only child at the time. When my father came home from prison, he was all beaten up. Then I saw how Jews were beaten and synagogues were burned. So I got some kind of ambition for revenge. The only way I thought I could avenge myself was by being a Zionist and helping Jews get to Israel. In my home Zionism was so pronounced, there was no difference between religious and political Zionism. There is only one sort there. All the Jews in Aleppo want to do something. All the Jews were in fear all the time. They're just waiting to do something.

"I was about twenty-one when I got involved. We were on our own, just a group that came together, organized. We had a few Arab friends to help. We also had contacts with Jews abroad in Turkey. They bribed the Arabs. The Arabs had to be paid. We were volunteers. The Arabs used to take the people physically and guide them across the border. The first time I was caught I was caught with two Arabs. The second time, one of those two was the one who betrayed us. He was just a crook, or perhaps he got more money from the authorities. I was caught smuggling Jews in the summer of 1964 and was sent to a civil court, not a military court. Then I sat about two months in prison. I was arrested twice after that.

"The second time I was in prison was from 1965 to 1969. The one Arab who was caught with us the first time betrayed us the second time. They caught one of the busses full of people ready to leave for Lebanon. The Arab arranged for the bus to the mountains near the border. Usually, we used to take the people to the mountains, then take them across the border by foot. This time when the man betrayed us, he took all of us to a place and told us to wait. 'There are more people coming to join you,' he said, 'and you'll all cross together.' Then he went and called the police. They just let the women and children go. The men all went to prison.

"It was very hard. I was tortured, beaten, over every part of my body. The military police wanted to know who our contacts were abroad. During interrogation, they used electric shock. I was dipped into cold water in winter. I was arrested in June, Friday before Shabbat. When they imprisoned me, the local newspapers announced they had caught a new Elie Cohen.[10] In May, 1965, Elie Cohen was hanged. About two weeks later I was arrested, and they told me, 'We're finished with Elie Cohen. Now it's your turn.' They sent me to the same court that tried Elie Cohen.

"It was a military court, two officers and one civilian from the Ba'athist party. The prosecutor was either a military man or from the party. There were journalists present. The trial lasted about four months. I had an attorney, an Arab. His defense basically was, 'They tried to smuggle people out, but after all they didn't leave.' He gave as an example, if one goes to steal, but at the last minute doesn't enter the house, perhaps at the last minute he had second thoughts. Perhaps he would not have stolen. Perhaps those people didn't mean to go to Israel, but to another country. He asked them to set us free."

Almost anything but a superspy, Tsur was returned to jail. His punishment, sixteen years in prison, was reduced to six because the escape had failed.

"I had no uniform, nothing. I stayed with these same clothes for a year— winter, summer, everything in the same thing I came. There were times when we didn't even have underwear. We could wash once a week. Once in two or three months, we were allowed to shave. I have a beard. I could not see my family, not in four years. After a year, my family sent me clothes. Then maybe every six months or so, I was allowed to write a letter. When I remember this I cry.

"For a whole year were were in solitary confinement, each one of the whole group, in a small cell by himself. Two Arabs and six Jews. After one year all eight of us were put together in a big room, and then we were transferred to a small room. We did nothing, nothing. We just sat there. There was no place to exercise. We didn't know what was going on. Even during the Six Day War. We heard there were new prisoners, but we didn't see any.

"After forty months, we were taken out each day for about ten minutes. It was such a small cell, we couldn't move. We were one on top of the other. We slept on the floor, without anything. Nothing, just blankets, no straw. It was very dirty. Nobody cleaned.

"We weren't allowed any spoons. We were eating with our hands. Each one was given a plate with his food and after they finished eating, they took the plate away. The food was military rations. Mornings there was bread, tea, cheese, or olives, very few. About four or five olives if that was the day's menu. Lunch— rice or barley soup and a piece of meat. Evenings—potatoes or lentils, sometimes eggs, but just one. No coffee. That was the menu for the first year. Afterward, when we had contact with our families, we could buy better food. It was permitted. Also if the chief of the prison was in a good mood, he would allow it. If we were to be punished, he wouldn't allow it. Now and then the chief of the prison would be changed. There were those who wouldn't allow the buying of cigarettes. It was *asur* [forbidden].

"We were hit or shouted at all the time, day and night by the guards who wore the uniforms of the military police. There were some who were just indifferent. Many, though, were vicious. We gave them nicknames. Just cusswords in Arabic. The way they treated us was part of the nickname. The Arabs call themselves by the names of their sons—*abu*. There was one named Abu Raja and we called him Abu Wujjah because *wujjah* means pain in Arabic. He put out cigarettes on my shoulders. I still have the burn like the symbol of the Ba'athist party in the shape of a 'V' on my shoulder."

Tsur spoke softly and nervously smoked cigarette after cigarette as he recalled the torture chamber. "There was a room. It was soundproof. There were blankets on the walls. And on the floor they had iron loops. There were chains on the walls, a different sort. There were even some on the ceiling so the feet would be up. They used to tie the men with the chains, feet and hands. They couldn't move. And they would beat them. We were naked, but for slips, underwear. They used braided leather straps. We were given one hundred strokes with that whip. We used to be bloody.

"They used to bring a tire of a car or bus and put a person inside. Then they beat them. Another time, they put electric shocks to the fingers. They would bring this special machine with live wires and put it between fingers. [At this point, he demonstrated with his hands how the device worked.] There was a handle that used to make it stronger. And they would turn it to the degree they wanted.''

What medical attention the inmates of the prisons received was granted grudgingly. ''Once I was sick for two months, blood in my stools, and I wasn't taken to a doctor. Once in the middle of the night, we were going to showers. We all undressed. I was in solitary. I was waiting a few hours and it was terribly cold. We were taken to the shower and when I got back, I had a terrible stomach ache. I started to cry from pain. A guard outside had this little window to look in. He saw me and went to get his superior. He came and asked, 'What's the matter with you?' I had to stand at attention because he was an officer. 'Are you sick?' 'Yes,' I said, 'please help me. I'm sick. I have pain. I am going to die.' And so he just punched me in the face. 'That's all the aid you're going to get, dirty Jew. Lie down in your cell.'

''Once, I had a sore throat, a high fever. Every day, I asked to be taken to the doctor. After about a week or ten days, nothing was done. My whole group decided not to eat, to go on a hunger strike. They brought us breakfast—bread and tea—and we didn't eat. The commandant came and asked, 'What's the matter with you?' We said, 'We won't eat. Our friend is sick and going to die. If you don't help him, all of us will die together.' So he said, 'Okay you eat and I'll take him to a doctor.' That day he took me. And the doctor shouted at them. He was angry with the military police because it took them so long.''

Some of Tsur's comrades could not endure the punishment. ''Some of the guys were taken to the hospital, bleeding from the nose after being tortured with shocks. There was one fellow in solitary who was tortured in the tire. They hit him and left him bleeding from a cut near the eye. He couldn't take it. There was a nail on the wall in his cell. He took it out and swallowed it. They took him to the hospital and he came back a week later.''

Released in 1969, Tsur was arrested a third time in 1973. ''That was during the Yom Kippur War. Two of my cousins and another friend of ours ran away at the time, disappeared. So that's the reason they came and arrested people from the families. They thought I was doing it again. They came and arrested two of my uncles. They didn't take my father at the time. They wanted younger people. Old people were left alone. There were times when they took Arabs and Christians, too, because they thought they were helping. They arrested about twenty youngsters at the time.

''I was in jail just for a month. I was taken to a dozen different places where they interrogated me, different buildings in different cities (Damascus, Aleppo). Once I was chained for a whole week inside a cell. The chain was to the bed, so I couldn't get up for a whole week. At the beginning we were all together. But during interrogation everyone was singled out. When I got back from interrogation, I told everybody what happened. Many times I came back unconscious. Many times, I would faint and they just threw water on me and continued. At the beginning, I didn't say anything. Toward the end, I just told them about myself, not about the others. They didn't arrest anyone else in my family.''

Once again, Tsur's principal tormentor was Abu Wujjah, who delighted in reminding Tsur how he once had been equated with Elie Cohen. It was during these torture sessions that Tsur was burned with cigarettes. To this day, he does not know why he was released so quickly. Some of his Jewish friends remained in jail until 1980, the year that Tsur finally escaped from Syria. For seven years, he lived in fear as Abu Wujjah made it clear, "If I were caught again, they would kill me."

Freedom cost $6,000 in payment to smugglers, and $1,000 each for his wife, four children, and himself. Like many of the Holocaust survivors, he hopes one day to write a memoir. Yet there is a ring of ambiguity in his words. "I wrote when I was in jail. I wrote notes. Then before I was released, I was scared they would find it, so I tore it up. After I was released in Syria, I wrote it again. But then before I came here, I thought the same thing, so I tore it up again. When I came here I sat down and wrote everything again. Although I still have relatives in Syria, I don't think it's dangerous. What can they do to them? They are not responsible for my actions."

10

A Death at the Door

A sad, but persistent, theme in Jewish history is that regardless of the number of generations born in a land or the cultural contributions they have made, when the time comes for a government-sponsored program of persecution, Jews have been scorned as outsiders. What transpired in Spain, France, Hungary, and Germany has, to a lesser extent, been replicated in Syria. As one Syrian-Jewish emigré, responding to a question concerning how long his family had lived in that country, put it, *"Dorot* [generations]. Ask the *Muhabarat."*[1]

Like the Gamaliels, Hadlis, and Bahats, Rabbi Maurice Nissan found it necessary to flee his native Aleppo. What triggered his flight was the memory of an atrocity, which, like the Abadi affair, went relatively unnoticed in the international press. Surrounded by six children in a comfortable housing project in Tell Kabir, Israel, the bespectacled thirty-six-year-old rabbi (now a computer specialist for Bank Leumi) related his story.[2] "We have been in Syria almost five hundred years. From the expulsion of Spain until now, we are in Syria. I don't know what town in Spain, but my father told me that our family originated from Spain. My father was director of a Jewish school in Aleppo from 1922 until 1972, the same place, fifty years in our synagogue. He was a very, very celebrated man. All the people knew him. He was a very, very good man and a very good teacher. He was responsible for all the children in Aleppo.

"We are ten children, five boys, five girls. I was number eight. When I was a boy, I couldn't go to the street to throw balls, because we were afraid of Muslims. We had to stay in our house all the time, because we were afraid. You could not wear a *kipah* [skullcap] in the street because we were afraid of

Muslims. Many times they beat us in the street and ran after us to our house. Of course, I was beaten up as a boy. Our parents couldn't do anything and the police would not. We went to the police, but they didn't help all the time.

"All of the people there are afraid of the Muslims, always. In Aleppo there isn't Fatah in our neighborhood. But in Damascus, the Palestinians live together with the Jews, in the same house, each with two, three rooms. It is very difficult to live with them because they are *sonim* [enemies] to us. We are always afraid the Muslims would beat us, do something bad, all the time, and especially in wartime.

"My father told me what happened in 1947. They went to all the synagogues in Aleppo and burned the *Sefer Torahs*. They burned the school and things. After that, all the Jews were afraid to go out of their houses for days. The big synagogue in Aleppo, the historic one, they burned the *Bet Knesset Hagadol* in Aleppo. Some people told me that in history books it's said this synagogue dates from the time of King David. The first historic synagogue in the Middle East, two thousand years old. They did rebuild half of it.

"During the wars, they asked us to be in the house before nine or ten in the evening. We had to be there until five o'clock in the morning, until the time of prayer; 1967 was a very bad time for us. We just sat in the house and went out only to buy something to eat near the house. It was difficult. They called us bad names—'You dirty whores' and 'Dirty Jews, God will punish you.' My father was a handsome man and all the people knew him, even the Muslims. Fifty years, he was director of the school and every day he went the same way to work. My father had a tarboosh, a red hat.[3] Several times, the Muslim children took the hat and pushed him.

"In Qāmishlī, it was worse. They put the people in their houses for six months. Only the women were given permission to go out and buy something for a couple hours. In Qāmishlī, the people are poorer than any people, very poor. Only two or three families are rich. Lots of people left to live in Aleppo. There were twelve hundred Jews in Aleppo in 1980 and four hundred were from Qāmishlī. For six months, people in Qāmishlī sold things to get food."

Like his father, Maurice Nissan became a rabbi-teacher, working closely with Muslim supervisors. "I taught Hebrew and mathematics, French. I also did some decorative work with gold. I had a small shop. All Jews had a boutique. Some work with gold, some work with Arabs. They don't make good money, but it's enough.

"There were some Muslim teachers in the schools. We brought them because we didn't have a teacher of philosophy. We brought him for twenty hours a week, not full-time. The real teachers are Jews. We have a *menahel* [director] who is Muslim. He didn't interfere with what we did because we taught Hebrew in the synagogue, not in the school. In the synagogue, we could do anything. They knew what we were doing, but they left us to teach Hebrew in the synagogue.

"The police didn't do anything in the synagogues. Ten years ago, they went in to ask what we were teaching. We told them we teach only Torah and *Noviim* [prophets]. We don't teach *Gemara* [Talmud] because they hate Talmud and *Gemara*. But really, we teach Talmud and all sorts of things—*Halakah* [religious law], *Shulchan Aruch* [code of Orthodox Jews]. We had religious books, which came from Canada.''

Although the Assad government officially propagates the myth of religious toleration, there were problems. "Each book that came to Syria had to have permission from the *Muhabarat*. But we had friends. We gave them something—*shohad* [a bribe]—to take them in. I was the connection for the books, the first one in Aleppo to have contact outside to bring books, to help people go out of Syria. Sometimes the books or packages came to us torn, because they wanted to see what was in a strange book. We were supposed to translate from Hebrew (they were all in Hebrew, not French or English), but I didn't agree to this. I gave them a bribe and took the *limod* [scholarly manuscript], *mezuzah* [wall amulet], and other things away and I gave them to people who asked me for a *siddur* [prayer book].''

In times of crisis, Jews could not rely on Syrian laxity or venality. "When something takes place between Israel and Syria (war or another thing), the situation gets very bad. The *Muhabarat* takes people and puts them in jail and we have to report every morning and evening to the clerk of the *Muhabarat*. The *Muhabarat* reads every letter that comes from outside Syria. If they don't understand something, they ask the man to go to the *Muhabarat* and sometimes they put him in jail. They brought me once. 'What does this mean? What about this phrase? That is a secret phrase. That means you had relations with Israel!'

"We had a neighbor who was a poor man. His children were in New York, and they were rich. My father wrote to them to help their father. They had been my father's students. So the children agreed to send the money for their father. The *Muhabarat* read the letter and they see this story in this letter. So they ask my father to go to the *Muhabarat*. My father was seventy years old. They asked, 'Why did you have to do that?' More questions. They prohibited him from doing things like that again.''

Generally, Nissan viewed institutionalized anti-Semitism as an inconvenience that might, on occasion, be turned to the advantage of the intended victim. "I had an identity card marked *Mussawi*, in red letters. Not now, but we have to write *Mussawi*. Then years ago, all the people in Syria had to sign that line. Not today, I think it's better to sign *Mussawi* than *Yahudim* [Jew], because if anyone takes the identity card and sees *Yahudi*, he might do something bad to us. Many people don't understand what *Mussawi* means. Not everyone understands it means follower of Moses because they are not intellectuals.''

Noting a thaw in government policies over the past decade, Rabbi Nissan points out that Syrian Jews can own automobiles and telephones. Educational opportunities and medical treatment have also improved, with some reservations. "There are no restrictions about going to a university. Ten, fifteen years ago, they would not let Jews go to the universities at all. After that, Assad agreed

Jews could go. But if a young man is religious, he cannot *doven* [pray] because all the examinations are on Shabbat. So all the young men who are religious like me don't go to the university.

"As for medicine, there are a lot of doctors, all of them *prati* [private]. You can go to anyone you want. In Aleppo and Damascus, there are a lot of Jewish doctors. So firstly you go to a Jewish doctor. If it is necessary to go to a better one, he gives the name of a specialist. It's never a problem. Seven, ten years ago, if a Jew were sick and had to go out of the country for treatment, they would not give him permission to leave Syria. Now it's better. A lot of people come to New York, Europe."

There is, however, always the rub of guarantees and relatives. "When the government agrees to send one of the members of a family out, they ask him for a deposit—about five thousand dollars to eight thousand dollars. They give from one to the other. When they return, they get the money back. If they don't return [he laughs], the money goes to the government. They don't agree to let people go. They agree that one member of the family can go out. *Afilu* [even if] they put up a lot of money, they will not agree. Only one or two members. They have to leave members from the family in Syria because I think all the Jews in Syria are hostages. Assad one day will discuss exchanging them with Israel for Syrian soldiers. Perhaps Syria won't let the Jews go out because they are afraid that the Jews will come to Israel to help them in war. Because they speak Arabic very, very well, *neged* [against] terrorism, and other things like that.

"If I had parents in Syria, when I left, the *Muhabarat* would have taken them. If anyone had parents there, it would be very dangerous to flee because they take the parents, put them in jail for one month, two months, and beat them. But our parents were in Brazil. Father, brother, mother, were all out. I could leave Syria because I had no parents there."

Rabbi Nissan deliberated a long time before leaving Syria. As he put it, "I had to find a man who could help, someone I could rely on." Nissan was aware that the *Muhabarat* inveigled Jews into a trap. For seven years, though, he lived with a memory he could not erase, the murder of his brother-in-law Zakki Kasab.

The incident has been embellished through many tellings. In one form, Kasab was shot to death "before his family" by an Arab whose brother had died in the Yom Kippur War of October, 1973. "The murderer, who is well known, has not been arrested."[4] According to David Sitton, however, the crime was perpetrated by three men of Syria's "Second Office" in the last days of March, 1973. Having gone to question Kasab and finding him not at home, the three men "immediately" rushed to his father-in-law's apartment where they forced their way in, firing automatic weapons. When Mrs. Kasab came to her father's house, she found her husband's body lying in the stairway and covered with blood. "She caught a glimpse of the three men making their get-away in the car in which they had arrived." Although the Jewish community insisted on an arrest, the police responded, "the case was closed for want of sufficient evidence."[5]

Neither version is accurate. Rabbi Nissan was present when the murder occurred and this is how he remembers it. "In 1973, one week before I was married, I was in the house of my wife filling out wedding invitations. It was an apartment, four rooms, with thirteen people living in one apartment. My brother-in-law was there. *Ptum* [suddenly] there was a ring on the bell. My brother-in-law went to open the door and they killed him. The man who rang the bell shot him with a pistol and my brother-in-law staggered back to the room and said, 'They've killed me.' He died on the spot. After two or three weeks, this Muslim went to another Muslim and asked him to give him money and he told him, 'If you don't give me money, I will kill you like I killed the Jewish man.' This second Muslim was a good man and he went to the *Muhabarat* and told them this man killed the Jewish man two weeks before. They took him and put him in jail. After six years, they let him go. Only six years. I saw him before I escaped.

"He killed my brother-in-law because he was a Jewish man. The same day, he had gone to a Jewish doctor to kill him, but the doctor wasn't there. He was performing an operation. The doctor's children opened the door and told him the doctor was sick. Then they immediately closed the door. So he thinks, 'What can I do? The doctor is sick. So I go to another family to kill one Jew.' Only my brother-in-law (may he rest in peace) doesn't know this man, doesn't know him at all. So he came to kill him. And he left three boys, three small children, the oldest was nine, the smallest five. Now they are all in Israel and are soldiers.'

"If somebody else had answered the door—my father or me—of course, he would have shot us. He just wanted to kill a Jew."

In 1980, his parents safe, Nissan and his family escaped. Their journey to freedom was reminiscent of the Crusaders' passage through the Cilician Gates. "I left Syria with my family and another family. We were twenty-one people with nine children. I had four children and my wife was pregnant. We left Syria with some Muslims who agreed to help us escape to Turkey. We paid more than four thousand dollars to them to help us escape. We traveled in an auto about two or three hours. After that, we started to go by foot in the mountains, mountains that were very hot. It was very, very difficult for the children. It rained. It snowed. We had to throw everything (food) we had prepared away, because you couldn't carry it in your hands. We had to go and go and go in the mountains and all the children and women had scratches and cuts. We had to go without food, nothing. After twenty hours, the Muslims left us in the desert. They told us they would bring us food. They brought cheese and something else. That's all we ate. After that, we had to go two days without anything else. No water, nothing. The children asked me for a drink of water. We had an umbrella and opened it to catch the rain. We squeezed water from the umbrella. Finally, after about another forty-eight hours of walking, sitting, walking, sitting, without sleeping, all the children slept in our arms, they brought a truck to us from Turkey and we went to Iskenderun.''

To this day, Nisson ponders the risks of such a journey. ''The way between the two frontiers was very dangerous, very, very difficult. When we went across the frontier, it was very dangerous because all the Turkish soldiers were near the frontier and they had binoculars and could see us. If I had known in Syria that the way was like that, I wouldn't have agreed to escape. Really, I was in danger, with my family and another that came with us.''

On the day I spoke with Rabbi Nissan, his family was anticipating the bar mitzvah of their eldest son who had just celebrated his twelfth birthday. A time of joy and freedom without parallel in Syria where the *Jamaa*, Assad's ruling junta, winks at murder of Jews within its borders and where the *Muhabarat* has plotted the assassination of foreign critics. (A car bomb scheme in the summer of 1972 went awry.) Pondering the merits of any of Hafez al-Assad's successors—Foreign Minister Abdal Halim Khaddam, Defense Minister Mustafa Tlas, Chief of Staff Hikmat Shihabi, or the erratic Rifaat al-Assad, Rabbi Nissan echoes the concern of Jewish refugees when he says, ''I think that Assad is better for Jews than any other chief in Syria. If he died, Rifaat would be worse, and Khaddam or another would be worse yet. I believe if he died, there would be a pogrom.''[6]

11

Damascus: The Haret el-Yahud

Damascus has a fabulous past. Situated less than fifty miles east of the Mount
Hermon ridge, along the principal byways leading to Beirut, Homs, Hama, and
Ammān, this fabled city of silk has captivated travelers and conquerors throughout history. In September, 1918, Great Britain's Field Marshal Edmund Allenby,
on the urgings of Thomas E. Lawrence, permitted the forces of Emir Faisal to
"capture" Damascus and give birth to the myth of Arab self-liberation in World
War I. Centuries before, both Saladin (who repulsed the Third Crusade) and
Baybars (who stemmed the advance of Mongol invaders in the Middle East)
selected this city, which served as the center of the Umayyad Caliphate, as their
own capital. A provincial capital for the Romans and Persians in the pre-Christian
era, Damascus was the site of early missionary work by St. Paul. Tradition has
it that the prophet Elijah was fed by ravens in a cave at Djobar two miles outside
of town. The oldest continuously inhabited city in the world, dating back nearly
4,000 years and boasting a population of over one million, Damascus seems to
have learned little from history.

When sometime BBC correspondent Colin Thubron visited Damascus twenty
years ago, he found a people who were notorious for their xenophobia and
bigotry. Of the Damascenes, Thubron wrote, "They have a long history of
massacres. In the reign of Nero they slaughtered ten thousand of the city Jews
in a single day after keeping the plans hidden from their wives, who were mostly
addicted to Judaism."[1] After discussing the futility of reforms attempted by
French colonialists and Mehemet Ali that did not prevent the slaughter of Maronite Christians in the nineteenth century, Thubron wrote of the Jews, "Among
the minority peoples of Damascus there is no sadder community."[2] Once bankers

and absentee landlords, they were the principal objects of "the Damascenes' instinctive hatred [that] reaches back to the time of David and is now nurtured and artifically inflamed."[3]

Jewish residence in Damascus may date back to the time of the ninth-century Aramaean king, Ben Hadad, who was allied to Ahab of Israel in the struggle against Assyria and who guaranteed a residential zone for Jews in Damascus in exchange for similar streets in Samaria. At one time, 14,000 Jews squeezed into the square-mile Haret el-Yahud (Jewish quarter), which is located between the Bab Charki (Gate of the Sun) and Bab Kaysan (Gate of Saturn) on the city's southeast side. When Thubron visited the Jewish ghetto, it already was a depressing place. The streets, he wrote, "are very quiet. The doors of sunken courtyards are edged open and slammed shut to receive children from school. The walls are pocked and misshapen. Nothing is ever repaired."[4] The one cemetery was desolate and in the synagogue where Elijah supposedly anointed Elisha, an Arab schoolmaster stood before Palestinians, "teaching the children to hate."[5]

Conditions did not improve in the next few years when the Palestine Liberation Organization (PLO) group Al Fatah moved a unit into the ghetto. The homes remained the same ancient mud-brick hovels that served as workplace, kitchen, and dormitory for a single family; electricity was shut down at 9:00 P.M. Now, however, more stories filtered to the free world of Jews being terrorized in the narrow lanes where they lived. "Benching" (prayers after dinner) was forbidden, as was the blowing of the ceremonial ram's horn or shofar. In the spring of 1974, nine Jewish youths were kidnapped in the Haret el-Yahud.[6] Seven of them were murdered. About the same time, an Italian visitor reported that the Jewish cemetery had been razed, to accommodate a highway cutting to the airport. Parts of the cemetery were used as a training ground for the Syrian army. If Jews raised enough money, they could move their family graves to a small, adjoining area; otherwise the coffins were dumped into a common grave.[7]

Today, some observers offer that conditions are not that bad for Damascus Jews. Stephen Shalom, one of the few Americans to visit Syria on several occasions, has been quoted as saying the community was "Orthodox, vibrant, and enjoyed complete economic and religious freedom."[8] More recently, Shalom, whose father established a fund for the relief of Syrian Jews in the 1930s, clarified that position. "At no time are Jews discriminated against as a religion," he told me. "If you ask them what is the single most important issue, it would be schools. They are very well run in Damascus and Aleppo, but they need additional classrooms in Damascus."[9]

A more detailed, but comparable, assessment came from a Jew who, it should be noted, was about to return to Syria. This man sounded much like Selim Totah or Joseph Jejati, the prominent Damascus businessmen who were periodically trotted out to speak with Western journalists.[10] "Everybody wants to live in the ghetto. The houses are very old, stucco and block. You can't change them, they say, because they are historical. You're not allowed to build any houses or renovate them. Maybe after a long time, you will get a permit and maybe not. There are two-story apartments, with three families living in one building. There was a bakery under us. Each family has two or three rooms off a hallway open to the sky. There is electricity, water, although everybody, including Arabs, has none for five hours each day. Everybody has television. We watch soap operas, news, *Kojak, Dallas, Bonanza.* We have a number of big and small sofas in our living rooms because most people have large families so they sleep on the couches.

"It's not that dirty. The people clean, wash near the door. You're not allowed to use much water in the street because of rationing. There are some rats and mice, but no dogs. Dogs aren't allowed for religious reasons. They make too much dirt.

"There are Palestinians. We live with them. There are even some in the yeshiva now. It used to be bad. When we were growing up, they used to call us names and throw rocks. There was some difficulty in school. The kids would fight, the parents would fight. It's not so bad now. As for the Jewish cemetery, they did want to build a road to the airport in 1976. But they took part of both Jewish and Muslim cemeteries, only a part. It was a big cemetery. They transferred thirty-five hundred graves.

"The *Muhabarat* doesn't watch the bet knesset or schools. We have twenty synagogues and they are filled every day and Shabbat. The El Franj synagogue is two hundred years old, very big, in Arabesque architecture. We use folding chairs. Perhaps fifty or sixty come daily. We could accommodate three hundred. As for the shops, some of them are big. People sell clothes, jewelry, make brass. There are a lot of factories owned by families. The average income is around five to six thousand liras per month. Some make twenty-five thousand liras a month, about one thousand dollars. It cannot compare with America, but I think it's a very good living."

Others have a less sanguine view of conditions in the Haret el-Yahud. According to Moishe Cohen, head of the Israel Council for the Rescue of Jews in Arab Countries, Syria's aim in isolating Jews in ghettos is anything but humanitarian. "In Damascus, the Jewish community is concentrated in a very old quarter. And within this quarter, there is a station for the *Muhabarat,* the intelligence service of the Syrian army. It's easier for the Syrian government to control them. To oppress them, to torture them, when they have no social relations with other groups."[11]

Concerning economic activities, Cohen states, "At one time, some who dealt in foreign trade were very rich, especially in Aleppo. After 1948, the Syrian government started to restrict them, slowly, step by step. Beginning in 1967 there was no import-export because all communications between Jews and the rest of the world was censored. No trader wants every paper, every letter, he writes about his activities to be controlled. Instead, they work on a local level. In Damascus more of them work as artisans. Maybe eleven or twelve families

Arab children standing on ruins of Jewish cemetery in Damascus circa 1972. Photo courtesy of the National Task Force for Syrian Jews of the Canadian Jewish Congress.

are in a very good situation today. When [French President] Mitterand was in Syria, he talked with Assad about Syrian Jewry. And Assad told him, 'We're going to visit and you can see the stores of the Jews.'[12] In one large avenue in Damascus, there were three or four big stores. Not like an American or European operation, but large stores, boutiques. These Jews have their problems and must cooperate with the government because generally they are afraid. It's very natural that they would think of their economic activities. You see it all over the world. I'm not sure they would leave if they had the opportunity. They would not be the first to leave, but they would leave. They are not stupid. Don't forget what happened in Iran. The Jews stayed and after that they were hanged.

"Now about religious problems. Generally there is no religious problem. The Syrian government generally does not approach religion. First of all, the Muslim Brotherhood in Syria is a problem. And don't forget that there are many aspects of Islam and Judaism that are similar. It's also difficult for the government which is from a special sect of Islam—the Alawis. It depends what you mean by religious activities. For example, within religion there are many aspects of religious Zionism. That's forbidden because it's Zionism. For example, it is not forbidden to pray the *Shmoneh Esrah*,[13] but you can't learn the Hebrew language as a language. You can learn the language just to pray, as Latin for a Christian, just to pray without any comprehension. They don't know what they are praying for. If you look at that as a religious problem, I think it is, because you can't pray without understanding what you are asking God.

"The Jewish people have no relations with the civil police. They deal only with the intelligence service of the army. From time to time, in Damascus, the *Muhabarat* came to the synagogues and observed. But that's a very delicate point, and for this reason it seems the Syrian government is very intelligent. Generally, they don't talk about anti-Jewish activities. They don't publish that. When the Jews lived in Iraq, the Iraqi government had many laws against the Jews and published them in the official papers. In Syria's case, there is no need to publish the laws. Everything is very administrative. Once you create such laws, such tortures, then the Syrian people are afraid to contact Jews even if there is no law because they don't want problems with the intelligence service of the army.

"Are all the laws still alive? I don't know. Syrian Jewry has its ups and downs. Many times it was very difficult to be a Jew in Syria. Very dangerous. From '71, '72 to '77 it was very dangerous to live there. You know about the four young girls. They couldn't leave their city. No more than 5 or 6 kilometers. For the moment, they can travel. But you are still in prison. Even if this prison is of gold, it is a prison."

That same theme of an imprisoned pet, sounded by Rabbi Isaac F. in Deal, New Jersey, was echoed by another refugee who said of Syria's Jews, "They live like a bird. They can eat, live, study, work, and everything is all right. But they are in a cage and can't get out. The whole family cannot get out. Ask Assad why not. Nobody knows. Maybe if peace comes there can be an exchange."[14]

This individual, a dark, handsome man of forty-three, whom we shall call Elias, tells a different story of his native Damascus, where shortages exist in sugar and medical supplies, shoes and milk for babies, and water and electricity. Furthermore, it is a city where one-fourth of the families had no decent food for Rosh Hashanah 1986, and where Jews have been molested for their religion as recently as October, 1985. "At Simchat Torah, my brother was arrested. When he sang *Adonai Melech*, he sang it like *Hatikvah*. The people were upset because the *Muhabarat* took him to prison. The *Muhabarat* has a building right in the middle of the ghetto. A very nice house, maybe three stories. The Jewish community remodeled it. There are twenty men in the house. They patrol the streets all the time, watching the people. If you are arrested, they take you first to the ghetto *Muhabarat*, then to another station. We have so many prisons in Damascus—the Kalla is a museum, Adra is the worst. Nobody is allowed to see you. If somebody in the family tries to escape, maybe one or two times they accept it. But now if you escape, it is five years."[15]

Elias knows the Syrians' capacity for inflicting pain. In 1973, he was pressed into service, handling the bodies of Israeli pilots downed during the Yom Kippur War. "The *Muhabarat* came at night. We were instructed to bury the pilots according to religion in coffins. We had to go to a little town, Najah, and dig the graves. There were police all around. We had seventeen pilots to bury. The bodies smelled so bad. One of the rabbis asked the police to open the coffins, to see who was inside, but the Syrians said it was no good for the corpses. The rabbi, Ibrahim Hamra of Damascus, was so upset, he cried."

For the most part, Benjamin Z., the nineteen-year-old premed student from Deal, paints a similar, depressing image of Syria. The eldest of ten children born to a family of metalworkers ("it's a common profession over there"), he has few positive memories of his Damascus childhood.[16] "A child's life there is very different. You spend most of the day in school, from 7:00 A.M. to 5:00 [P.M.]. After 5, you go home and prepare your studies for the next day. In the summer, we all worked with my father, making trays, coffee urns, copper plates. There are some people, very few, who don't work in the summer. We were lower middle class. The youngest is three and one-half, a girl. She has a few dolls. Not like here. My little brothers have a few toys, some balls. Sometimes they play soccer. They work a little bit, go to synagogue.

"You are afraid of the people around you. You can't feel free. We used to live like that, an uncomfortable life. When we were boys we got into many fights. The Arabs went after me. Sometimes they beat me up. But I think the Palestinians who lived near us were very bad people. Their parents teach the little boys to hate the Jews. They don't like us and you can't say anything.

"I had a bar mitzvah. The custom is to have a party in the house. I had my bar mitzvah in the synagogue. I made a speech about why God gave us the Torah, why especially to us and not other nations. We had many rabbis. We learned Hebrew in school. There were two schools, one for boys and girls. The name of the school was Moishe ben Maimon. It was a very small stone building, maybe two or three floors, more than sixty years old. Every two or three years they made repairs. There were seven hundred or eight hundred kids in the school and when they made an application to the government to enlarge the schools, the government didn't agree.

"Even in schools, it's very difficult dealing with the teachers, dealing with people around them. The director has connections with the secret police. Many times the secret police are making problems. They come to school to check up what we are learning, how we are behaving. We learned Hebrew in the school. As far as I know it is forbidden in the school as a language. You can teach it like a religion. They were teaching us *Chumash* (Torah). Children can't learn everything. But we say, '*Baruch Hashem* [thank God], they're smart. They'll learn anyway.' "

Benjamin's schoolteacher was something of a legend in the Maimonides school. For thirty years Yaakov Khazzan had been a teacher of mathematics, French, Hebrew, and Arabic in the school operated by the Alliance Israelite Universelle. Many of the Jewish teachers in this and other schools in Syria had been his students. He endured the trying times in the early 1970s when the *Muhabarat* came and stood by his lectern as he instructed his classes in Arabic. Today this likable, burly man is cautious with his references to life in Syria and bitter when he speaks about his new life in Israel. "None of the Damascus Jews really want to talk. I could write volumes. I went every day to the *Muhabarat*, millions of times. I did all kinds of things then. Why should I speak now? It's a very delicate matter. We all still have relatives there. I still have brothers, father, mother. Several weeks ago, there was a public demonstration in Tel Aviv. I was given a certificate from the Israeli government as a prisoner of conscience, like the Jews of Russia. There were photographs of the demonstration in the newspapers. My father and mother were interrogated. Their intelligence knows everything that is going on. Those who talk cannot envision what will happen. The *mishtara* [police] know what is happening. They pick up the papers, take the people and torture them. Of course, they torture."[17]

Khazzan lived among the winding alleys of the Haret el-Yahud, which he likens to the Jewish quarter of the Old City of Jerusalem. He experienced the ebb and flow of Syrian discrimination. "A long time ago, it was bad. There is a difference between 1948 and today. Today it is much better, except you can't go out. We hit back if they hit us. In the war [1967], there was great fear. People stayed in their houses. In 1970, 1974, it was bad on the streets. Today, *Ashaf* [the PLO] bothers a little. But the government intelligence is strong. Assad wants to be friends, wants Jews to stay. He hates Israel so bad he'll give everything they want, except going out. He hates Israel more than anyone."

Khazzan reciprocates that venom. "I hate Assad because he won't let Jews out. I spent thirty years working for the Jews of Syria. Three times, I was arrested. Once I was sentenced to six years in jail, another to twenty years, but I served only one month each time. The third time, I was sentenced to fifteen years and was in jail ten months. They arrested me because I was always doing things for other people. When I was in jail, my family had nothing to eat for a year, no food, no support. My two-month-old baby, there was no milk for him.

My wife came to the jail and complained why did I have to work for others and hurt the family.''

After this third time in jail, Khazzan decided to take his family out. On medication for nearly a year from the effects of torture, he nevertheless openly petitioned the *Muhabarat* for permission to emigrate. His application was repeatedly turned down. Then one night in 1985, he, his wife, and seven children abandoned everything (house, automobile, clothes) and crossed the border illegally. Pulling on his neck, Khazzan says, ''We came out only with our souls.''

Despite all he endured at the hands of the *Muhabarat*, Khazzan is almost wistful about life in the old country. ''I love Israel, but no one helps here. No one helps me to get a job teaching Hebrew, Arabic, mathematics. I was told when I came here, I would have to start all over with a low salary, no tenure. You cannot keep a family on three hundred or four hundred shekels. The *ulpan* [language seminar for immigrants] wasn't much help. My children don't have jobs, cannot go to the university. We have been staying five months in an absorption center, Kfar Chabad. There are about one hundred units, maybe sixty to seventy people from Damascus, five hundred from all over. A week ago, I took a test in accounting. But *ayn kesef, ayn avodah* [without money, there is no work]. If I had stayed in Syria I might have been pensioned by the government by now.''

Unemployed and bitter at the time of this writing, Khazzan's ambivalence about his decision to leave Syria touches on another moral issue raised by Rabbi Isaac F., of Deal, and Rabbi Nissan, in Tel Kabir: escape is only the first stage in achieving freedom. Without a major, sensitive program of rehabilitation, training in the United States, Canada, and Israel, many Syrian Jews operate in anomie. Like German refugees of the 1930s who infuriated social workers with their *Bei-uns* references (''Back home we had this and that''), they feel ignored and betrayed, and they wonder whether it wasn't better after all in the familiarity of the Damascus ghetto.

12

Qāmishlī

Al-Qāmishlī seems to be nobody's child. Located 450 miles northeast of Damascus, 300 miles from Aleppo, where Iraq and Turkey abut Syria, Qāmishlī is the smallest, poorest, and most remote Jewish community in Syria. An estimated 120 to 300 Jews still reside in this city, which has no fine neighborhoods or international trade like Aleppo and no great shops or synagogues like Damascus. Qāmishlī has one small synagogue served by a rabbi who commutes every fortnight from Damascus. When the rabbi, who doubles as *shochet* (kosher butcher), is not present, private individuals must perform the ritual of shehitah themselves. Qāmishlī has no professional *mohel* (circumciser) and no Jewish school. Jewish children attend the state school. In time of war, curfews are rigorously imposed by a government that counts among its worst enemies not merely Zionists but the Arab Ba'athists in neighboring states as well. Relations with Iraq deteriorated in 1975 when the Syrians moved ahead with their Euphrates Dam project.[1] Since then, the borders in this corner of Syria have swarmed with troops. For the Jews of Qāmishlī, so tantalizingly close to Turkey (no more than five or ten miles), it means that if they want to escape, they must somehow get to Aleppo or Damascus.

It is a far cry from the stone huts of Qāmishlī to the Gilo Absorption Center outside Bethlehem in Israel. Perhaps as many as 20,000 immigrants from Syria, Russia, Rumania, the United States, and Ethiopia are bunched together in housing that ranges from stark concrete bunkers on this strategic hill to more elaborate apartments for the affluent. The children attend school in a modern facility. They run and play together amid slides and swings, which punctuate the development. And their parents meet to discuss common problems and to learn new skills in a sleek community center operated by social workers from the city of Jerusalem. It was in Gilo that I interviewed seven Jews who once lived in Qāmishlī.

Albert and Ora Jamila live in one of the prefabricated units that seem to be stacked one atop another like so many railroad cars. He is a dark, slender man, whose father came to Qāmishlī from Turkey after World War I. She is a tall, buxom blond with blue eyes. They met when she was a teenager, and after a brief courtship, they were married in 1976. ("When a young man wants a girl," says Albert clapping his hands, "the sooner the better.") Albert's father, who had been involved with a number of unsuccessful enterprises with wheat and sheep, died in 1950. The couple eventually fled Syria in 1984. Today they reside with their five children in Gilo. Sparse though their furnishings and personal possessions may be, they, like relatives who live in a unit nearby, are grateful to be in Israel.[2]

Albert began their story. "When I was about ten, there was a Jewish school, to study Hebrew and *tefilah* [prayers]. They also taught French and Arabic, but nothing on Israel. In the public school, the only thing they taught about Israel is that they are all criminals and terrorists. Even in the books, Israel is put as Palestine. And the poor Palestinians, they are all in rags as refugees, to show what the Jews do to the Palestinians. We learned about Israel from snatches on radio *Kol Yisroel*. It was illegal to listen. In 1967, they collected all the radios from the families so they could not hear."

Ora added, "They closed the Jewish school. There is only the government school. No Hebrew, the textbooks are Arabic. Arabic geography. Israel is only Palestine. No Israel. *Asur* to talk about Moses, Yaakov, *Tanach*. We had to learn religion—either the Christian or the Muslim, so I picked out the Muslim, about Muhammad and the Quran. They teach the worst things about Jews and Muhammad."

One of Ora's sisters-in-law obtained a degree in mathematics from a Syrian university and was teaching in the public shools for more than a year and a half when she was summoned to the main office and fired. "Don't you know?" asked the director. "You're a Jew. You're not supposed to be working in a public school." As a young girl, Ora experienced similar anti-Semitism. "We used to have special military uniforms, like *Gadna*,[3] for occasions when visitors came to school. All the girls had to be dressed up in this beautiful uniform to show them how we're learning arms. But I was a Jew. They wouldn't permit me to wear the uniform. I was forced to stand aside. The visitors asked, 'Why is she not dressed like the other girls?' They explained, 'She is a Jewish girl.' Now it happened a second time that the visitors came, they didn't like it that a girl was set aside. So they made me put on the uniform [a khaki uniform with a peaked hat], but not to try the shooting, no drilling, just to include me."

The Jamilas could rationalize all sorts of discrimination as Albert told about life in Syria. "You can study, learn anything you want, but it is very difficult to get a post with the government. For example, if one graduates from the university and goes to the Ministry of Commerce he won't get a job. To be a policeman or a member of the armed forces, just a serviceman not in intelligence, would be next to impossible. There is no compulsory service in the army, but we did not think it was discrimination. If you buy a house, you can't sell it. Once they find out you are selling, 'Why are you selling? There must be a reason.' So they start to tail you.

"Normally, there is no trouble from the police, quite the opposite. They used to stand outside our doors to take care that we should not be disturbed by people who had sons, soldiers in the army. During the wars with Israel, in 1948, 1956, 1967, they were the furious ones who wanted to attack Jews. People who had sons that went off to war would say, 'Our sons have died and these people live!' The police intervened to take care of us so we shouldn't be attacked.

"If you wanted to move from one city to another, they would give you special permits. If you had to work in another city, you had to have the special permit besides your identity card. Only Jews, not Christians. To protect them from others. You had to have a reason to travel. You couldn't just go and say I want to travel because of a possible disturbance. You must bring a reason to army intelligence, the *Muhabarat*. If you have permission, nobody would interfere because people are afraid just hearing the word *Muhabarat*. When Assad came to power, he canceled all of those things and only the identity card was needed.

"The *Muhabarat* will bother you only if they find out you are trying to run away. If they find out someone is thinking of running away, they investigate them. For example, once about ten o'clock in the evening, a man who did not identify himself came to my home and started asking questions, investigating for the *Muhabarat*, trying to find out whatever they can. They would ask such things as, 'Is Israeli intelligence in contact with you?' At times, they would take someone, accuse him of a hundred things and throw him into prison where they would beat him for quite a few days to find out whether he really intended to run away. If they found nothing, they let him go home.

"There was one Jew by the name of David Moishe who was friendly with an Arab man. I mean he was a good friend of his. Some other Arabs went to the government and informed on David Moishe that he was preparing to run away. And this cost him one and one-half years in prison."

Albert's older brother Yosef was arrested under similar circumstances on three separate occasions. As a young man of twenty-seven, he was detained for two months in 1948 during Israel's War of Independence. He was rearrested while working as a custodian for a Talmud Torah in 1968, and again in 1973. A jovial, white-haired man who wears a Pinky Lee-style hat, he bears the scars of *Muhabarat* torture on his feet and belly. "In 1968, two or three persons were put in charge, to make certain the children shouldn't leave school. One of our students, a boy seventeen or eighteen years old (now he is here in Israel) ran away from school and fled the country. In the evening when they found that the boy was not at home, they caught him and said, 'You're responsible. You helped him to run away.' I was the oldest man who worked in the Talmud Torah. In school, I used to feed and clothe the students, give them pocket money, for twenty-three years. That's why they probably took me. I was put in a big tire, and had a helluva time because this young man fled. For seventeen days, another man and I were interrogated, beaten, stretched. 'Why didn't we inform that the boy ran away?'

"In 1973, the *Muhabarat* took us to prison because my neighbor fled. They said, 'You go to prison because you did not inform us that your neighbor fled. It is impossible that he left the house and you did not realize he had fled.' They tortured me—my hands with electric prods. They tied up my feet and beat them like a bastinado. Later, when I was taken before a judge, I asked, 'Why do you detain us?' When the judge saw that the evidence was not enough, he set us free.''[4]

The Jamila family could endure indignity, but not Syrian racism. Albert recalled,"They all hate the Jews, all the Muslims and Christians. There were some who were neighbors and were well acquainted with us. They treated us nicely. Most know the Jew as a criminal, a killer. 'They robbed everything from the Palestinians.' I heard this for the first time when I was young and in school. Whenever we passed by, some would say, 'You Jewish dogs!' and laugh. When two Arabs quarreled and they just had a good fight between them, one used to tell the other, 'Why are you fighting me so hard? Do you think I am a Jew?'

"Some of the people hate Jews, the same as they hate the pig. The Christians were even more of a problem. They used to say on the holidays how we butchered Christians while we were making bread for the holidays.

"I used to work with a very prominent advocate. This advocate had a ten-year-old boy. They learned so much about the terrible Jews in school, they are so bad, that the boy asked his father, 'Please, I want to come to your office and see how a Jew looks. Is he like us or is he different?' There are cities where there are no Jews. And whenever they find out there is a Jewish passerby, they used to run away. 'This is a Jew! Oh, my God!' To flee, the sooner the better.

"Once I was traveling from Aleppo to Qāmishlī, and during the trip there was a control or check. I showed them my identity card. On it was written *Mussawi, Bene Moisheh.* The guard didn't understand what the meaning was. So he went to his chief and asked him, 'What is the meaning of *Mussawi?*' He said, 'It means he is a Jew.' 'Do you mean to say that he is a Jew?' So a number of people came to look at us. All of the people were just as if they were up against a projector. This is a Jew. This is a Jew.

"I worked with an Armenian in 1967. The owner didn't know Arabic so well. So I was the one to deal with the customers. Two women came in and wanted to buy goods. While we were speaking, they asked me, 'What are you? Christian or Muslim?' I said, 'I'm neither. I am a Jew.' They said, 'A Jew? We don't buy here.' They left the place and ran away. The owner asked, 'What did you tell them?' I said, 'They asked what I was and I told them a Jew.' He got angry, 'Why did you tell them that?'

"During the 1967 war, I was working with this same man. There was a neighbor next to us in the next shop. He used to say, 'You remember. There is war with Israel. If the Arabs win, all of you are going to be slaughtered.' ''

An equally depressing view of life in Qāmishlī was offered by Rima Azur, one of the more recent arrivals in Gilo. A dark-haired, rough-faced woman who seems older than her twenty-seven years, she works in a candy factory. Both of her parents are dead and she lacks skills and education; she came to Israel alone and frightened in 1985.[5] "There was no *bet sefer* [school] for Jews, only for Muslims and Christians. Very few Jews went to the Muslim school. Some of the teachers were offensive and some were not. Jews were passive about insults. They didn't want to fight. If a Jew wanted to study in Qāmishlī, he went to synagogue. They used to teach them Alef Bet a little bit. Then later on, when they grew up, they sent them to Aleppo, only the boys.

"I didn't go to school at all. We worked all day in the house. We had a very small house, two rooms. From the time I was five years old, I worked in the kitchen, washed clothes. Some children had toy cars, bicycles, games like *cheshbesh* [backgammon] and cards. There was plenty of candy, chocolate, wafers. I don't remember having any dolls. There was fear of intermarriage, fear of assault. We weren't allowed to go to work because we had to pass through an Arab section. We stayed at home and did cooking, housework. I had no hobbies.

"There were no *hugim* [holidays], no social activities for teenagers. Learning Torah was the only thing in the *Bet Knesset* [synagogue]. The boys would gather at the synagogue to learn a little Torah, only boys. There were some films, sometimes on television, American, French. Alain Delon, Charlie Chaplin, *The Love Boat*. But we had no dreams about being a teacher or a doctor. We just talked about leaving Syria.

"Life over there was not good. We use to pay extra money to our neighbors to go and get food in the *shuk* [market]. We paid 50 percent of our earnings to the government. Not officially. The Arabs paid less. The *Muhabarat* would blackmail us: 'If you don't give us, we're going to have you arrested.' So we had to pay money to these people. If one person was missing from the count, the entire family would be taken to the police station where they would be beaten.

"When we had a war, there was curfew, all the time. We weren't supposed to go outside. We had to stay in all day. They used to count the members of the family to see if one was missing. The police, *mishtara* without uniforms, would come into every single house to count. Children used to run out secretly to buy whatever they could before the police caught them. If the police caught them they were beaten. One of my cousins was caught and beaten. He stayed in bed one month before he recovered.

"People in the neighborhood used to tell us, 'Go away. Syria is our country. You go back wherever you like. Syria belongs to us.' I waited for an opportunity, then I went to the border with Arabs. I had a visa to Turkey, not Israel, which cost fifteen hundred dollars. The money came from a family in the U.S.''

Rima Azur says she came to Israel because "I wanted to come back to my roots." She has other reasons, however. Cheated of her youth, she hopes one day to be a mother in her own house. And she works hard raising money to liberate her family. "I still have a sister and brother, with five children there," she says. "I am trying to raise the money for them to come out, perhaps ten thousand dollars. With the Arabs, he doesn't have much work. He makes coverlets, bedspreads, and after he does the work, they don't pay him what they owe."

Albert and Ora Jamila eventually managed to move to Aleppo, leaving her parents in Qāmishlī. Their first attempt to flee the country was aborted in 1980 when it appeared that the *Muhabarat* suspected their plans. Four years later, in November, 1984, they sold Ora's wedding ring and bracelets to raise the necessary $500 per head needed to pay the smugglers who took them, in the middle of the night, across the plain from Aleppo. And although they came to Israel "penniless, without clothes, nothing," they have no regrets. "We were afraid," says Albert. "I wanted to save my wife and family. We wanted to feel independent and come to Israel as Jews."

Among the seventeen Jews who escaped together was their sister-in-law Aliza who now works part-time as a teacher in the Maaleh Adonim settlement near Jerusalem. Each morning she takes two buses to reach the school, but she is not troubled by the inconvenience. "I never felt it was wrong to have ambition, to want to be more than a mother in a home. *Lo maspik.* It wasn't enough. I wanted more, more, to develop my mind."

Yosef Jamila and his wife also escaped in this group. When asked if he would ever consider returning to his native land, Yosef laughs and says, "If I were paid thousands of dollars, if I received all the treasures of Syria, I would not go back. Here is the Garden of Eden."[6]

13

Feminine Destiny

Herzlia Lokay is a thin, dark, energetic woman who lives in an exquisite apartment on Hatzalbanim Street, down the lane from Baha'i Temple in Haifa. Married to a Polish Jew, she came to Israel in 1952 as part of Operation Ali Baba, which brought more than 100,000 Jews from Iraq. As a youth in 1948, she learned firsthand that Arab brutality was not limited to Jews living in Syria. In a speech before the World Organization of Jews from Arab Countries (WOJAC), she remarked, "I acted as a leader of a group of girls in the Zionist underground Hechalutz in the town of Irbīl near Mosul. I was captured at the age of sixteen for my activities, jailed. During six months, I was kept as a prisoner in a men's prison. There was no women's prison in my town. During all that time they interrogated me with blows and torture. They wanted me to reveal to them the names of Zionist leaders. I never did. My trial was in Baghdad in a military court. I was not allowed any defense at all. Neither was I allowed to say anything. I was sentenced to two years in prison.

"In the women's prison in Baghdad, they took off my clothes and dressed me in a sack, a real sack full of lice and dirt. The director received me with blows and a shower of spit. The section where I was imprisoned was full of criminals and whores, many of whom were touched with syphillis [*sic*]. Blows, kicks, spit were almost a daily occurrence [*sic*]. But worse than this was the hard labor. From morning till night, the prisoners were made to wash the dirty clothes of all the prisoners in the men's section and in the hospital. My only comfort were a group of communist women prisoners, young, mostly Jewish, who were sentenced for long periods in jail. They were intelligent and pleasant girls who opposed Zionism, but liked and took care of me.

"In view of the humiliating conditions, the crushing laundry work, the tricks and thefts of other prisoners, and the danger of infection from them, the whole group decided to proclaim a hunger strike. 'We are political prisoners and should get special treatment,' said the spokeswoman to the warden. 'We demand bettter conditions, and an end to the laundry work.' 'Strike, strike,' mocked the warden. 'You'll die of hunger. We want to get rid of you anway.' Food was brought to us three times a day, but we didn't touch it. Kicks and curses didn't frighten us. And we accepted no persuasion, even from prison doctors and directors.

"On the third day, came the cops, 30 of them with clubs in hand. They dragged us to a room, closed the door, tore off our clothes, and for an hour they beat us until their clubs and boots were dripping with blood. We were left bleeding, swollen, blue, with many limbs broken. But we wouldn't break. For days we sat half asleep with apathy taking over the hunger's place. More tricks and threats followed. None would do. On the 15th day, three of us started fainting and we were taken to a hospital. There they tried to feed me through the mouth and with injections. But with my last powers, I refused. I was told the others did the same. On the 21st day, they tied me up, and with the nurses holding me, they shoved a pipe through my nose and into my stomach and pumped in the mixture. The same day, all the other girls were force fed. But the struggle paid off. Almost all of our demands were met—no forced labor, separate cell [sic], books, visits, cooking and food possibilities, clothes, everything. We organized studies and reading.

"But the director didn't forget me. When I started with cramps and fainting spells after the long strike, she sent me for observation. Only when I reached the place, I realized it was a place for mental cases. I started screaming that I was not insane and luckily for me was heard by a Jewish doctor who sent me back to prison. After a year and one-half I was freed. Although under constant watch, I continued with my underground activities until we left for Israel. When we came to Israel, they gave us a tent in Pardess Hanna and told us this is your home. After a few months, we received a cabin made of tin. The facilities and water were shared by hundreds of people, we have to remember these were very far from the conditions we had in Irbīl. We accepted this with joy as we felt safe."[1]

Committed to building bridges between Arabs and Jews, Lokay's first volunteer activity when she came to Israel was to work with Arab and Druze widows. Later, she helped organize language and homemaking classes for women at Haifa University. Today, Lokay serves as chairman of the Women's Division of the Labor party in Haifa and lectures on a variety of subjects for the army, kibbutzim, and high schools. Her consuming passion is the rescue of Syrian Jewish women that they might fulfill what she terms their "feminine destiny."

"The biggest question is that there are at least four hundred unmarried girls, célibataires, between the ages of eighteen and fifty there. The reason is that the young men went out and they haven't got anyone to marry. This means that some of the women have no alternative but to marry Muslims. Not willingly.

They are forced by the Muslims. I'll tell you how. Usually the Muslims are looking for Jewish girls. Such a boy cares for her. She has no way to reject him. No money, no other possibilities. So, *b'seder* [okay] she gets married. As a woman she doesn't want to be unmarried till she gets old. Several have married Muslims. There are cases of people taking girls off the street. I can't say for 100 percent. There are cases where kidnapping happens, not rape. The difference between forcing [someone] and [that person being] willing to marry is very slight. When a Jewish girl marries a Muslim, the parents go to the *mishtara* and complain. The police say, 'What are you saying? He loves her, they love each other. What do you care?' After, they never see her again. In the Orient, this is the case."[2]

This gloomy assessment is sustained by other observers. According to Moishe Cohen of the Israel Council for Rescue of Jews in Arab Countries (formerly of WOJAC), "Most of the Jews who escaped from Syria were boys for whom it was an adventure. For a girl, it's rather difficult to give a smuggler money and arrive safely in Cyprus or Turkey. A case in point is that of the four Jewish girls from Damascus. So there are many young girls still living in Damascus and Aleppo and they cannot find a husband to marry. That's a pure Jewish feminine problem, a tragedy."[3]

The Israeli author Amnon Shamosh, himself a refugee from Aleppo, agrees. Asked by a *Jerusalem Post* reporter why more women had not fled Syria, Shamosh responded, "The same smugglers would rape and kill them. There were a few girls who tried and we know how it ended. So the boys leave and the girls stay. There are hundreds of surplus Jewish women in Syria today with no way of getting married, having children, living—because life for a woman from the Orient is family and only family. So these women are buried alive. Their only chance is to become Moslem and marry a Moslem."[4]

Where others might be content to shed tears and utter poetry for Syrian Jews, Lokay decided to do something. What prompted her to action was a massacre perpetrated not in Syria, but in Baghdad in April, 1973. Five members of a Jewish family—Reuben Kashkush, his wife, two sons, and one daughter—were machine-gunned to death in their house at midday. Only one daughter, who had run out into the street, survived. Former Iraqi security chief Nazem Kazzar acknowledged that one of his police units had carried out the executions as "an act of vengeance" following an Israeli raid on Beirut that month. The Kashkush family had been due to emigrate from Iraq only two days after they were murdered.[5]

For Lokay, whose husband's family had perished at the hands of the Nazis, it was the Holocaust all over again. Less than a month after the massacre of the Kashkush family, on May 11, 1973, she wrote her first letter on behalf of Syrian Jews to Doris Jainsfeld, chairman of the Women's Committee for Soviet Jewry in Great Britain. There followed a deluge of appeals to officials all over the world. She says, "All of this, I did on my own, without an organization behind me. Whenever I heard something or met someone, I would send a letter or telegram. When Begin came to power, I sent him a letter. Two years ago, Haifa University held a very big congress on feminism. I wrote out a stencil for all the people calling for help to the Jews of Syria. Wherever there is a crowd, at all meetings of NAMAT (Pioneer Women), the biggest organization in Haifa, I open this question.

"I am a member of the Labor party and several years ago, I was on a mission to Europe. When I was in France, I met Gaston de Fer, the mayor of Marseilles, later the interior minister. We talked of many things, among them my story, the story of the Syrian Jews. He asked details, that I should write him. He was the only one seriously interested in this question. I wrote him a detailed letter through the mayor of Haifa, Arieh Gur'el, who was a good friend, and he forwarded it to the President François Mitterand. And Mitterand promised to do whatever he could on this question. When Mitterand was in Israel two or three years ago, I wrote Prime Minister Peres. I have connections with Peres and he talked with Mitterand about it. *Ayn shum* feedback."[6]

Nothing came of those appeals in 1983. But a decade earlier, Lokay did shake up the U.S. State Department. One week after the murders of the Zeibak sisters and Eva Saad, on March 10, 1974, she cabled Henry Kissinger appealing on behalf of the remnants of both Iraqi and Syrian Jewry. After reciting her personal history of torture at the hands of the Arabs and saluting Kissinger for his intervention on behalf of Israeli prisoners of war, she appealed "as a mother and an Israeli" for him to bring up the urgent question of Syrian Jewry during Israel-Syrian talks of separation of forces "before it would be too late." On April 5, 1974, Lokay received a response from Carol C. Laise, assistant secretary for Public Affairs; it read

Dear Mr. [*sic*] Lokay:
  Secretary Kissinger has asked me to reply to your recent comments regarding the murder of four Jewish girls in Syria. We have appreciated your interest in this matter, share your concern for the Syrian Jewish community after this needless loss of innocent lives. Syrian Security authorities have arrested four members of a band of professional criminals and charged them with the murder of the four girls. These men will be tried according to Syrian law. While we deplore the mistreatment of any peoples because of race or religion, this particular issue is an internal Syrian matter which does not seem to warrant U.S. intervention since Syrian authorities apparently are seeking justice.[7]

This sterile and inaccurate response, so reminiscent of heartless communiqués issued by government personnel during the days when Kissinger's own kinsmen were being written off as an "internal matter" for Nazi Germany, was paralleled by a limp (and unfulfilled) promise from U.N. Secretary General Kurt Waldheim to Abba Eban that he would intervene on behalf of Syrian Jewish women.[8] The Israeli newspaper *Davar* highlighted the embarrassing correspondence prior to Kissinger's meeting with Anwar Sadat that month. "Until I published in the newspapers at the time of Kissinger, nobody dared to talk about it," says Lokay. "They said it's not good to publish it. Shh. It's a secret. You shouldn't talk, shouldn't publish, shouldn't do anything about it. My opinion was you must make noise about it. After this, we heard that things were easier for them, in the interior. They still wouldn't let them go out. But inside, at home, it was a little easier.''

From her home in Haifa, this woman kept up a barrage of letters, to four U.S. presidents. When Jimmy Carter passed through Israel on his way to a Damascus meeting with Hafez al-Assad in May, 1977, Lokay sent a cable to the U.S. Embassy in Tel Aviv calling on the president to intervene for 500 women so that they all could leave Syria "in order to fulfill their feminine destiny." A similar appeal was sent to President Ronald Reagan on September 1, 1981. A response sent by the embassy on May 9, 1977 typifies the official U.S. position. Charge d'Affaires Thomas J. Dunnigan wrote,

As you know we're very much aware of this problem and have already raised it on several occasions with the Syrian government. We continue to be concerned over the special humanitarian aspect of the case you raise. We will neglect neither it nor the question of the status of the Jewish community in Syria. I wish to assure you that we assign high priority to all questions of human rights, especially to reducing acts of discrimination on basis of race, creed, color, sex, personal beliefs, wherever they may arise.[9]

The vaunted human rights policies of the Carter administration offered new hopes and allies in the struggle for freedom. Early on, speaking to the General Council of the World Jewish Congress, Carter sounded a personal debt to the teachings of Judaism and expressed a sensitivity toward "the memory of Jewish persecution and especially of the holocaust [sic]."[10] Administration spokesmen Cyrus Vance and Warren Christopher echoed their leader's commitment to the preservation of peace and social and economic progress.[11]

With the United States' retirement from Vietnam, Congressman Stephen Solarz, an outspoken critic of involvement in Southeast Asia, directed his energies to the question of Syrian Jewry. It certainly was legitimate, because Solarz's congressional district in Brooklyn probably numbered more Syrian expatriates than any other. In 1975, Solarz was among the first Americans, other than supple-spined television journalists, to tour the Damascus ghetto. Two years later in January, 1977, he returned, leading a delegation of U.S. Jews that included Stephen Shalom. This time the trip consisted of visits to all three Jewish centers, including Al-Qāmishlī. On his return, Solarz met with Secretary of State Vance and suggested that Assad seemed ready to accommodate the Jews.[12]

When President Carter dined with Assad in Geneva that spring, there was no public mention of Syrian Jews. The opening ceremonies were taken up, for the most part, with Carter toasting his "new friend" Assad as a "brilliant," "frank," "quite modest," "strong," and "enjoyable companion" whose "willingness to reach out to other people has been demonstrated by the trust which the Palestinians have placed in him, by his sacrificial effort to bring peace to Lebanon, and by his effort to bring about a closer relationship with his neighbors, particularly in Jordan.''[13] Assad, Carter's man of peace, returned no unction, preferring instead to repeat what he had said at the time of the Yom Kippur War. In light of his treatment of minorities in Syria and of Syrian operations in Lebanon and elsewhere, it is worth quoting at length.

We are not lovers of killing and destruction, but we defend ourselves against killing and destruction. We are not aggressors and have never been. But we have defended and are still defending ourselves against aggression. We do not want anyone to die, but we defend our people against this. We love freedom and want it for ourselves, as well as for others. And we are on the defense so that our people may enjoy freedom. . . . We are advocates of peace. We endeavor to secure peace to our people and to all peoples of the world. We defend ourselves in order to live in peace.''[14]

Somehow, through all this blather, Carter or his aides did, in fact, raise the issue of "the Jewish maidens." Emulating Soviet promises concerning human rights and reunification of families, Assad conceded that his government would permit some women to emigrate, but only those who had bona fide marriage proposals. Initially the number was set at fifty, and although the necessary documents were quickly obtained with the assistance of U.S. ambassador to Syria, Richard Murphy, and his deputy, Robert Pelletro, the Syrians backed off their pledge. "We got together fifty marriage proposals from men in the United States saying they had seen pictures of these girls," says Stephen Shalom. "They were of the same traditional faith, prepared to marry. We got all the seals, notaries, city, government, state. More stamps and ribbons than you could believe and sent them to the Syrian government. Then the foreign ministry permitted us to bring out only fourteen. None of the girls were to go to Israel. And they insisted that proxy marriages be performed before the girls left.''[15]

The deputation of U.S. Jews returned to Syria late in July with their list of the women between the ages of sixteen and thirty in hand. The proxy weddings took place in a small chapel of the Damascus Jewish school. With several hundred people, including agents of the *Muhabarat*, in attendance, Stephen Shalom "literally sweated off several pounds."

No one, not the Jews or the police, was deceived about the nature of these marriages. Few, if any, were to be consummated. For the women, however, the excitement was just as real as if this were the event they had waited for all their lives. One of the fortunates, Stella Farah recalls, "It was very exciting. Some of the girls wore regular wedding gowns. I wore pants and a blouse. Each marriage ceremony took perhaps two to five minutes. Rabbi Hamra presided and Selim Totah, the head of the Jewish community, stood in for the husband. Each girl would come up, and after, he would give her a coin. There was no celebration, food, singing. The *Muhabarat* knew it was phoney.''[16]

There was more excitement when the fifteen women (including one widow) and several children departed from Damascus on Air France and when they arrived at JFK on August 11. In addition to the press and relatives, social workers from HIAS (Hebrew Immigrant Aid Society), NYANA (New York Association for New Americans), and *Bikur Holim* were at the airport. The women were whisked away to religious houses where they stayed, four to a room, under rabbinical supervision, while they learned English and were given rudimentary training as secretaries, seamstresses, and pressers.

For some, the dream of freedom and motherhood has been fulfilled. Stella Farah now lives in a magnificent gray stucco home with two cars, a color television, and a VCR in Ocean Parkway. A maid from Guatemala helps her with her five children. Others have not been so fortunate. According to Jeanette Cattan, one of the social workers at *Bikur Holim*, the biggest problem for these women is dowry. "Girls cannot get married unless they have a dowry, real money, anywhere from six to twenty thousand dollars. She has to come up with the money for the man. People helped the girls of 1977. Many people wanted to help. Fathers borrowed for the dowries. But when more came out, the help stopped. Sometimes a girl will date three or four men to see which she has the best chance with. I'm not talking about love, money. It's not unusual to have a marriage postponed the night before because of money. The divorce rate is low, even though they do not marry for love. They may sleep in separate bedrooms, but they remain married. There are a lot of girls in their twenties or thirties who are spinsters, some in their forties. They have a lot of problems. They don't trust anybody. They lie about where they are living. You have to understand their experience in Syria. They get very depressed. All of them come out with some problems. They get sick after all the stress. One woman told us, 'You are my parents.' "[17]

Two of the girls who came with the initial group in 1977, the youngest, could not cope with life in the United States, the noise, the dirt, the rush of subways, and the lack of safety. Stella Farah is somewhat sympathetic. "There's a big difference between life here and in Syria. There everything is very close, tight-knit with the families."[18] After several months in the country, the girls decided to return to Syria. It was 4:00 P.M. when Steve Shalom, who was in his office, learned that the girls were about to leave. He rushed to Kennedy Airport and boarded the plane in order to convince them not to go back. "I pleaded with them to no avail," he says. "Since then, I've thought it over and am sorry I met with them."[19]

In 1977, Assad promised Carter that he would continue to let Jewish women emigrate for the purpose of marrying their coreligionists. About the same time, U.N. Secretary General Waldheim was promising Menachem Begin an intervention to reunite members of 800 Jewish families. Although some sources maintain that Syria has carried out its pledge and that the pool of marriageable women has shrunk from 500 to 150, others argue that like the Soviet Union, the Syrians have reneged. Some people indicate that only a trickle, no more than ten or fifteen women, have been permitted to leave for matrimony in the past decade. If that is so, then the problem must still exist, because Sherry Hyman of the Joint Distribution Committee points out, "Nearly every woman of marriage age in Syria has four or five children."[20]

Meanwhile, Lokay continues to write to President Reagan "to let those miserable women leave Syria in order to get the opportunity to live decent lives and be able to fulfill their feminine destiny." She speaks for WOJAC rallies in Paris, London, and Ramleh, pleading "to help free the five hundred Jewish women in Syria who still are living in horrible conditions, who cannot get married because of the lack of Jewish men."[21]

Lokay views Syrian Jewry as part of a greater tragedy. "The entire world speaks about the Palestinian problem," she says. "We from Arab countries came to Israel also as refugees. We lost homes, money, billions, ten times more than the Palestinians, only from Iraq. Did we do any harm? Israel was a new state and absorbed every Jew that was a refugee. Iraq and other states had oil, money, and they did nothing for their own refugees." She has little patience for the many Jewish organizations that have been chartered to support the Jews of Syria and that spend much of their time and energies in ego conflicts. "Everyone wants to be in charge of their own organization. The problem is that the Syrians don't organize. Those who came to Israel through the years are not like the people from Russia or anywhere else. They fast, they go to the Wall, they strike, they do everything. There are many names among the Syrian Jews, but no leaders. They spend all the time praying in the bet knesset." To those who counsel quiet diplomatic intervention, Lokay retorts, "The first thing is to rescue them. Why did [Anatoly] Scharansky get out? Because every day people from the U.S., Thatcher, Reagan, everyone said, 'Scharansky, Scharansky, Scharansky.' If you keep putting on pressure, something good comes out. It should not be too late to save lives. We must do something now. Later on, we can light candles. Don't give Assad a moment of rest. He says that 'in my country there is freedom for everyone.' Every day, every hour, there is no freedom. Every opportunity, tell the members of the British Parliament and Congress. Every time. I'll do everything. I'll turn the world upside down for the Jews of Syria."[22]

14

Conclusion

At a London conference of the World Organization of Jews from Arab Countries (WOJAC) in December, 1983, a representative of Syrian Jews expressed gratitude to President Hafez al-Assad for lifting various restrictions and giving Syrian Jews "a certain sense of security," though without changing their status as second-class citizens.[1] In August, 1987, free-lance journalist Laura Veltman, having just returned from a trip to Damascus, concluded a piece on Syrian Jews by suggesting that Jews were as well off as any minority under President Assad. "In fact," wrote Veltman, quoting a British diplomat, "the Jews are in many ways better off than the Palestinians."[2]

While such statements infuriate some individuals engaged in rescue work, others, concur with the assessment. "If you talk to the Jews in Syria," says Steve Shalom, "they will tell you the situation improved with Assad coming to power in 1972. They are thankful to him in that respect."[3]

For the most part, Syrian refugees allow that Assad made it possible for them to own telephones and automobiles, eased off religious surveillance and public harassment by the police or Palestine Liberation Organization (PLO), and enhanced educational opportunity and health care. This 1980s thaw in government policy notwithstanding, there is no mistaking the *dhimmi* status of Syria's Jews even today. Few Jews advertise their existence by displaying *mezuzot* on the street entrances of their houses. In a land where the annual per capita income is less than $1,000, the *Muhabarat* still require a deposit of $5,000 to $6,000 for any Jew temporarily leaving the country. Amnesty International continues to report two or three human rights abuses each year from those Jews hearty enough to speak out. For as Veltman writes, "Winkling out someone who would actually talk about what it was like to be Jewish in Syria today proved, however, a tricky business."[4]

Not everyone who speaks positively about Assad is a Pollyanna. Rabbi Isaac Dweck is the spiritual leader of one of the largest congregations in Deal, New Jersey. One of ten children, he fled with his family from Aleppo in 1960. In 1977, Rabbi Dweck returned to Syria for the first time as part of the U.S. delegation working to facilitate proxy marriages. He, too, noted Jewish endorsements of Assad and improvements in living conditions. "We went from synagogue to synagogue with people blessing Assad," Rabbi Dweck stated. "He is from a [Shiite Alawite] minority and that's why conditions have improved."[5]

"There is some difference between 1960 and 1977," conceded Rabbi Dweck. "You cannot call it freedom. There is no freedom of expression. You are not allowed to learn Hebrew. Then, Jews were harassed. It was common for a Jewish child to be hit on the way to school, for glass windows to be broken. We were taught a course on Arab Palestine in school. Later, there was an Arab principal. A lot of laws affected only the Jews. A Hebrew print shop with a long tradition was closed up. Now, the *Muhabarat* is in charge of the Jews. They are not being beaten. There are no burnings of synagogues as there were before. There are opportunities for work. Kids can go to the university. Some travel is permitted outside the country if you deposit a large sum of money and not all relatives go out."[6]

Still, Rabbi Dweck is not so naive as to suggest that conditions have moderated all that much. "There is constant fear," he said. "You never know what tomorrow holds. Fear—you get used to it. It's constantly there. The people are living, existing. No freedom of conscience. No free speech. Free travel. No such thing as human rights. The right to vote? [He laughed.] What good would that be in Syria? You have no right to complain to the police. If a low-level official of the *Muhabarat* slaps you or tortures you in jail, you have no right to complain. I suppose there is medical attention—there are several Jewish doctors—but you never know as a Jew what to expect when you're being treated in a hospital. All the people fear when Assad will fall, it could be more serious if the Muslim Brotherhood takes over."[7]

Virtually everyone agrees that Syria denies its Jews the basic freedom of emigration in order to keep them as a bargaining chip in its dealings with the state of Israel. "The government of Assad is criminal," says David Sitton, president of the Sephardic Community in Jerusalem. "He is pressing on them, using the Jews as hostages. They know Jews are sensitive. They know that when Hezbollah and others begin to kill them, the echo will be heard all over the world. Jews from America will send money for papers, smugglers, and Assad takes it. This is the kind of government we are talking about."[8] Sitton believes that mass petitions and government interventions (particularly from Canada or the United States) have impact on the Syrian government. Ammon Shamosh has a slightly different view: "Congressmen and MPs make speeches demanding

that Assad let all four-thousand four-hundred Syrian Jews go. Well, he won't
do it. If I were Assad I wouldn't let them all go either—they're useful to him
as hostages."[9]

Perhaps the clearest assessment of many issues comes from Moishe Cohen of
the Israel Council for Rescue of Jews in Arab Countries. There is, for example,
the diplomatic or political aspect of the problem. While granting that Syrian
Jews, like their Soviet counterparts, are being held as hostages, Cohen makes
distinctions between the two situations based on the Arab-Israel conflict. Whereas
all Soviet citizens have restrictions on their movements, he points out, only Jews
are restricted in Syria. Three million Jews in the Soviet Union constitute an
important minority, with great researchers and savants. It may even be argued
that despite its totalitarian nature, the Soviet Union cannot be oblivious to the
scrutiny of a Western press or human rights monitors. Hence, a few *Refuseniks*
such as Ida Nudel or Anatoly Scharansky are permitted out, to boost the Soviet's
image of *glasnost*. Syria is a different story. Its government is not necessarily
responsive to public opinion. Jews in Syria "have no economic power, political
power, or scientific power." Unlike the Soviet Union, Syria fears that its Jews,
once free, might emigrate to Israel, as so many have done, and strengthen that
state in its ongoing conflict with the Arabs. Cohen said, "If President Assad
declared that every Jew who wanted to leave could do so in forty-eight hours,
I'm sure more than fifty percent would leave the country in two days.[10]

Like Herzlia Lokay, Cohen views the problem from a second or feminine
perspective, the right of women to marry and have families within their own
culture and tradition. Apparently few feminists outside the Jewish community
share this concern. When Cohen's aide, Ora Schweitzer (herself an Egyptian
Jew) presented the U.N. International Women's Conference in Nairobi, Kenya,
with a resolution urging that Syrian Jewish girls of childbearing age not be
deprived "of the most elementary human right—that of motherhood," in July,
1985, she and other Jewish delegates were hooted down with chants of "Out,
out, Zionists, out!" Schweitzer wrote, "The most vicious accusations were
hurled at us, some so preposterous that a Hebrew University professor, experienced in international 'meets,' broke into tears when she realized she had been
made use of in a 'Peace Tent' set up for the purpose of vilifying the United
States and Israel."[11]

For Cohen, there is a broader, third dimension that he labels the community
or human rights problem. "Even if the Syrian government regarded them as
citizens," he said, "there would still be problems. Every time there is a war
between Israel and Syria it has an effect on the Jewish community. This was
the case in 1948, 1956, 1967, 1973. A few years ago, they had the special
identity card marked with red. For the moment, *Mussawi* is written in blue ink
or typed in." Any opportunities for education, employment, or medical attention
are all restricted. "If a student is in philosophy or arts, that's okay. If he wants
to be doctor or pharmacist, then he has to deal with the intelligence service, fill

out a questionnaire, be under their control. If you finish a practical faculty, engineering, you can't work. Jews can't be employees in the government. Even if they study at the universities, they can't work.[12]

There are some additional aspects to education,'' Cohen continued. "We have a booklet on education in Syria concerning Jews. You can see there many aspects of education against Jews, Judaism, and Zionism. Not only does Syria teach anti-Zionism (maybe she has to because she's at war with Israel), but she also teaches anti-Semitism. Posters. Declarations of the ministry of education. How can a Jew be educated in such an environment? It's tragic.''

As for health, Cohen said, "To my knowledge, there is no problem in this area. If someone is ill today, he can go and have all the care he needs. We must mention, however, that medicine in Syria is not so sophisticated. Once any Jew is ill and he needs to travel, don't forget he can't go out. In the last two or three years, many Jewish people received passports to go to Europe or the States to have medical attention. To receive this passport, which was good for only one time, they had to give the government something like three to five thousand dollars. They have to leave their family as hostages. There's no problem for Christians.''

To say that Jews leave Syria to obtain medical attention is an overstatement. The Assad government may be sensitive to public outcry, but there have been incidents of victimization of innocents, such as that of Shimon Khabash, in recent years. There is, for example, the case of the Lahti family. In 1983, the father took ill with Hodgkin's disease and, strapped to a stretcher, was permitted to come to New York with his wife and year-old baby. A four-year-old son was held back. Subsequently, the family received letters from doctors indicating that the boy was ill and needed treatment beyond the capabilities in Syria. Relatives had four separate meetings with the *Muhabarat*, who periodically promise that the boy would be out in three or four weeks. Shalom has raised the bid for the boy's freedom from $5,000 to $10,000. Three and a half years later, the answer was still "no soap."[13]

Even more heartrending is a tale told by Judy Feld Carr. In May, 1985, she arranged to have a seven-year-old girl who suffered from a heart condition leave Syria. "She may have been a blue baby," says Carr, "but she received no proper treatment.'' Another substantial bribe was paid to obtain passports for both the girl and her twenty-year-old sister, because the Syrians would not permit the mother or father to accompany the child. Carr had been in touch with the little girl, who was on her way to Israel for an operation. Carr packed her own trunk with toys and gifts for other refugees in Israel ("Four of my families had babies," she said), and she carefully added the one object that the little girl had requested: a Cabbage Patch doll. The girl never received the doll. Three days after undergoing surgery at Hadassah Hospital in Israel, she died.[14]

Carr bitterly told me, "I couldn't even notify her parents that she had died or where, to let them sit *shiva* [a period of mourning for seven days observed by religious Jews]. These were Orthodox people. *Shloshim* [thirty days of mourning are also required] will be up tomorrow, June 28. Her parents can only sit in mourning for two hours afterward.'' To those who suggest things may not be that bad in Syria today, Carr snaps, ''How could anybody go back where you cannot go out in the street without fear of being beaten or raped? How can a little girl play with her friends or relatives, where your father is afraid, where there is no future?''[15]

''Mrs. Judy'' continues to send prayer books, tefillin, and *mezzuzot* to contacts in Syria. (Authorities imposed a $250 import tax on these goods in September, 1986.)[16] Those Jews who attain freedom, leave Syria with little more than the clothes on their backs. All of them bear physical or psychological scars. As Jeanette Cattan of *Bikur Holim* pointed out, ''All of them come out with some problems.''[17] And some, like the young girls who decided to return to Syria, cannot cope with the stress of a different society.

In the United States, agencies such as *Bikur Holim*, HIAS (Hebrew Immigrant Aid Society), and NYANA (New York Association for New Americans) attempt to help with the readjustment to a normal life, but they have mixed success, as the Gamaliel family testifies. In Israel, a small group in Jerusalem has spear-headed the relief programs. Formed in 1979, the *Irgun Nashim Lman Hasochnut* works with hundreds of families in the impoverished districts of Gilo, Talpiot, Katamon, Baka'a, Yir Ganim, and Kiriat Menachem. The government provides housing, but a handful of volunteers, lacking any continuing budget, must come up with clothing, bed linen, pots and pans, refrigerators, and even dolls for the children. (When one of my companions, Yedida Hadaya, gave a simple, celluloid doll of the kind you find at Coney Island to a little girl, it was as if Hadaya had done the greatest mitzvah.) Miriam Meyouchas, a zaftig middle-aged woman who traces her Sephardic ancestry to Romania, has been the spark plug of this group. She explained, ''As they arrive in Israel after passing the borders illegally, leaving behind all their property and belongings, they are in great distress, especially as they have large families—with four to eight children. We are active with social workers encouraging women and children to take educational pro-grams, learn English, take special courses, seminars, gymnastics. We pay the costs to the community center, arrange lectures on medicine and science, gyne-cology, nutrition, psychological problems. The hospitals give physicians. Hundreds attend these lectures. Sometimes the fathers come also. We give stipends to gifted children who want to go to a conservatory to learn to play some instrument, to youngsters who want to participate in recreational camps during their vacation, to girls who want to go on to secure a teaching certificate or other skills. We provide the tickets every month on Egged. Some have to take as many as two or three buses each way. We mobilize for the holidays, for Passover, supplying dishes and other things. Some don't need help, but some have nothing.''[18]

Like Lokay, Meyouchas realizes that Syrian Jews who live in the free world must organize and do more to help their brethren. ''Right now, we are trying to organize the new immigrants together to form a Union of Syrian Jews. Amer-

ican and Canadians in Israel have an association where veteran immigrants help
newer ones. We want the Syrians to help themselves in a positive and creative
way. We don't want to do it, but to help them organize.''

Meyouchas works closely with the Sephardic Council in Jerusalem. Sitton,
her superior, views the issue of Syrian Jewry as part of a larger question—the
reclamation of a proud Sephardic heritage. Once considered the elite of world
Jewry, Sephardic Jews resent being labeled Orientals. Even more, they resent
the Ashkenazic cultural focus that shunts aside the achievements of Maimonides,
Judah Halevi, Moses ibn Ezra, and Solomon ibn Gabirol. Sitton, a picaresque
character born in Jerusalem in 1909, points to a recent issue of the monthly
journal *The Battle* in which Dr. Ruth Feur asserted the need to reconcile the
bias of European Jewish history with that of all the people.[19] "Twenty-five years
ago, we decided that many things were being ignored. In 1951, we established
the World Sephardic Federation with branches in all parts of the world. We
attract many communities who were far from the idea of Zion or nationalism.
Our rabbis went to Bokhara. They didn't know anything about Zion and they
received them. Sixty years ago, they began to come to Israel and they established
this new quarter in Jerusalem under the influence of this rabbi.''[20]

The Sephardic Federation has had an impact on the government of Israel,
forcing its Department of Education to reconsider its treatment of this community
in schools and textbooks. Under the direction of Dr. Avraham Chaim of Hebrew
University, the research center Misgav Yerushalayim has sponsored three international conferences, underwritten research proposals, and published numerous
works of scholarship ranging from a study of Judeo-Romance languages to short
stories of Jews from Iraq.[21]

Sitton swells when he talks of ten volumes of Spanish *niggunim*, *hazzanut*
(religious chants), and liturgies that have been recently published. But he is
especially proud of the historic and humanitarian achievements of the federation.
"Our community is the oldest in Israel. It has existed for seven hundred years.
One hundred thirty years ago, we established the first Jewish hospital in Jerusalem. Why? Because the missionaries were attracting Jews. They were leaving
the Jewish tradition. So the rabbis established this hospital near the Hurve Synagogue, a new building. It was destroyed in 1948 when the Arabs took the Old
City. We wanted to rebuild it, but the government said no. They wanted it out.
We intend to rebuild it with one hundred beds, all kinds of medicine. Up to
now, we have invested about three million dollars that a few people have collected.

"We have relations with communities all over the world and mobilize them
to help. Those who first opened the gates of Russia were under our influence.
We were the first to fight for the Jews of Ethiopia. Fifty to sixty years ago many
Sephardic Jews visited Ethiopia and came into contact with them. We are doing
our best to save the Jews of Syria by any means. We are receiving them. We
are giving scholarships. This year, we gave seventy thousand dollars to seven
hundred students from all kinds of universities and secondary schools. The way

to help our nation is to educate the new generation, especially those who came from backward countries. Till now we have educated thirty-five thousand students in the past forty years. You cannot imagine how big a role they are playing in the life of Israel—some of them judges, managers. We issue releases in Hebrew, organize press conferences. Two months ago, there was an international meeting in Paris to support Syrian Jews. Our representative Netanyahu called on the U.N. to tell the Lebanese and Syrian Jewish hostages to be free and not be killed just because they are Jewish. When the government organized a meeting on behalf of the prisoners of Zion from Russia in Tel Aviv and awarded honorary certificates to the sister of Ida Nudel and others, several Syrian Jews from Gilo were also honored. Every day on television, when the prime minister talks of the Jews of Russia, he mentions the Jews of Syria. All the time. Before, he never discussed the matter. It means now we are a factor."[22]

Self-congratulations of the sort offered by Sitton may be premature, because 4,500 Jews continue to wallow in the prison that is Syria. Historical circumstances are never precisely the same. The very existence of the state of Israel has altered the world's perception of Jews. But I maintain that there are disturbing parallels between the present situation in Syria and that of Nazi Germany during the 1930s. Despite differences in numbers, there was a Jewish minority that had resided in the homeland for centuries, yet was regarded with xenophobia. Identity cards clearly marking them as Jews have been mandated and people have been harassed by paramilitary goons on the streets. Their children have been humiliated in schools, their cemeteries vandalized, and their synagogues objects of arson. Professionals have been ousted from their positions, access to trade and education have been restricted, and censorship has been imposed on communication with the outside world. Jews have been segregated into dilapidated ghettos where their movements can better be regulated by secret police. Attempts at escape, particularly with currency, are illegal. Offenders have been arrested and tortured in filthy prisons where inmates might be forced to wear the same suit of clothes for a year or more. Whole families or communities are held collectively re-sponsible for the actions of one person. While leaders wrestle with their personal responsibilities to their people—whether to flee or stay—the oppressive govern-ment warns the free world not to meddle in its internal affairs. Furthermore, Syria has offered haven to unrepentant Nazis such as Alois Brunner, who recently declared, "All of them [Jews] deserved to die because they were the devil's agents and human garbage. I have no regrets and would do it again."[23] And while some counsel not to publicize a situation that refugees label *rak pachad* (only fear) and while some fret about where to send the refugees or how to apportion credit for their rescue (until it may be too late), others warn that if something is not done immediately, pogrom will soon supplant persecution.

"People don't understand," said Shalom. "Everybody in Syria is afraid of what will happen after Assad. Muslims say, 'Just wait. We'll get even when Assad goes.' If there is a pogrom, it would be very bad."[24] For Shalom, Rabbi

Nissan, Rabbi F. and all the others, Hafez al-Assad is no friend of Jews, but he is preferable to what might come after. Whatever changes he made in Syria resulted from internal concerns and external pressure. The fifty-seven-year-old president, who has already suffered several heart seizures, cannot live forever. Once he goes, Syria may come under the control of a more extremist rule of a sort posed by his brother Rifaat, the Sunni Muslim Brotherhood (20,000 of whom were purged by Assad at Hama in 1982), or a Shiite faction aligned with Khomeini. The effect on Syria's Jews would be devastating.

All the more reason to press Assad to let these Jews go. Like Rabbi Stephen Wise and Ze'ev Jabotinsky before him, who traveled through Europe's prewar ghettos reminding their kinsmen they were not forgotten, Shalom's trips to Syria have been inspired by the need to "be as visible as possible." Three such exhausting trips and several State Department interventions since April, 1985 have failed to produce a face-to-face meeting with Assad at which Shalom hoped to raise the issues of reunification of families and a reduction of *Muhabarat* brutality. Shalom's conclusion is the same one offered by Rabbi F., Rabbi Nissan, Herzlia Lokay, and Mr. Elias: "We need to go public as in the case of Soviet Jewry."[25]

Cohen agrees. "The ups and downs of Syrian Jewry," he says, "was not by *hazzaz* [celestial trumpets]. It seems that the pressure of public opinion all over the world creates these 'downs,' when times get better. Press the Syrian government or the Syrian ambassador. Press on your representatives in the States, in the government, in the Senate, in the Ministry of Foreign Affairs, in UNESCO, the United Nations, in religious institutions, in the unions. If you press these activities, I think Syria will think twice before doing anything to Syrian Jewry. Maybe they will ameliorate the situation. I don't believe in amelioration. Amelioration is to let them go. That's all Assad has to do, declare that all the Syrian Jews can go out. If they don't want to go, then all the people all over the world should shut up. We think it could be a very good idea on the basis of union of families to let them go. Many have families living in the States, Brooklyn, Los Angeles, South America, Brazil, Argentina, Colombia, Chile, Panama. For me it doesn't matter if they arrive in Israel or the Diaspora. The point is that they have to be free."[26]

Freedom through reunion with families is still the declared policy of both the United States and Canadian governments. Also the French government, whose Prime Minister Jacques Chirac made a promise several years ago, when he was mayor of Paris, that he would not visit Syria until the situation of Jews there had improved. For some Jewish leaders, however, that is not enough. Sounding much like their vainglorious predecessors in the Holocaust, they quibble about the destination of Syrian refugees. "There is a question of philosophy," said Sherry Hyman of the Joint Distribution Committee. "Some people feel that if the refugees come out under the sponsorship of Jewish organizations or money, they should settle not in the U.S. or Canada, but in Israel, that the Israelis have the best perception of the problem. The feeling in Israel is that Assad is using them as hostages and the Israelis won't be blackmailed."[27]

The problem with this approach is that until recently, Israel had no official policy on the issue of Syrian Jewry. Candles were lit and Sephardic leaders were invited to offer touching phrases during days of national mourning, but the government declined any public statement that might rebound against Jews remaining in Damascus, Qāmishlī, or Aleppo. People actively involved in ransoming Syrian Jews sneered at governmental hints about secret rescue efforts. Only in 1986 did the Israeli Knesset pass a formal resolution decrying the harsh treatment of Jews in Arab lands. At the same time, Ambassador Benjamin Netanyahu, speaking before a WOJAC conference in Washington, conceded that the government of Israel had neglected the problem of Jewish refugees from Arab countries.[28] Acknowledging the unlikelihood of direct negotiations between the Zionist state and Syria, Cohen urges greater effort on the part of humanitarian organizations outside of Israel. "We expect Jewish organizations all over the world and organizations who are fighting for human rights to be more active than us," he said. "If we talk, Syria would say they are talking about hostages. But first of all, it is our duty. They are our brothers, mothers, fathers."[29]

For forty years, the world has worried over the fate of Palestinian refugees. Resolutions have been adopted in the United Nations recognizing their inalienable rights and statements of concern were issued by the Vatican. More than one billion dollars have been contributed by democracies to UNRWA (United Nations Relief Works Agency) for relief and rehabilitation work and perhaps another $100,000 to a war chest by members states of the Arab League. The PLO enjoys quasi-diplomatic status in many nations and its supporters have the ear of Western journalists whenever tires are set aflame in the streets of Gaza or Nablus. By way of contrast, Syrian Jews, like their counterparts from Operation Ali Baba or Operation Magic Carpet, must rely solely on the generosity of Jews in the free world. In the United States that means the Ronald Feld Fund of Beth Tefiloh, Baltimore, Maryland, and in Canada, the National Committee for Jews in Arab Lands. Beyond these two small charitable funds, there are tears and poetry.[30]

There may well be a time when Syrian Jews, given an opportunity to leave the country, will, for whatever reason, remain behind, just as a handful have done in Libya, Iraq, and Yemen. Jewish tradition holds, however, that there is no higher obligation than *pidyon shevuyim* (redemption of captives). In the Middle Ages, communities mortgaged synagogues to save their kinsmen in far-off lands. If we have learned anything from the Holocaust experience it is that we must move heaven and earth to redeem those in peril, to prevent a re-creation of the Holocaust. On a smaller scale, to be sure, but one that will nevertheless be as cruel and deadly. Today it is Syrian Jewry. Tomorrow, it may be the Jews of Iran or Morocco. I am speaking of the beautiful blond child munching on a banana in an apartment in Jaffa, the twelve-year-old son of a rabbi in Tel Kabir, the Ethiopian children in Gilo who spoke better Hebrew than I, the chubby woman who wanted to be a schoolteacher, the four brothers from Aleppo, one of whom escaped via a submarine, and the beautiful daughter of Mrs. Gamaliel in Williamsburg. They are not aliens. They are not different from us. They are not Syrians, they are not Sephardim. They are Jews. They are our people and we must help.

The minimum action commanded of decent people includes

1. Petitions to government representatives, the United Nations, the International Red Cross, and the Vatican such as those issued by Soviet Jews (Josef Begun, Vladimir Slepak, and Alexander Joffe) to Brezhnev in 1972 and Jacques Chirac in 1987[31] urging pressure on the Assad government to abide by the terms of the Universal Declaration of the Rights of Man.

2. Financial support to groups that feed, clothe, and send religious articles to the Jews of Qāmishlī or Aleppo; financial support to those who bribe or rescue; and more financial support to those agencies left with the unglamorous task of rehabilitating refugees once they have attained freedom.

3. Unabashed demonstrations, academic symposia, oral testimonies, and publications, as much to buoy the morale of the unfortunates trapped in Syria as to inform the free world.

From that darkest of all eras, the words of the Polish-Jewish poet Leib Olitski still ring true.

> All men are brothers and each people is my own.
> My Jewish people, though, of ancient stock and fame,
> of you, I grew, a gleaming spark at first unbeknown;
> but drawn to you the spark rose and became a flame.
> When enemies their dusty storm against you raise,
> I set against it, turning to the sun, my Jewish face.
> When dark-grey clouds upon your head descend,
> I stay with you, my people, to the end.[32]

Postscript

February, 1989. Several months have passed since I participated in the special conferences on Syrian Jewry in Ottawa and Montreal. If it can be believed, the situation has actually deteriorated in that time. Although several specialists in the Israeli Foreign Office have pleaded, "The American-Jewish community has to do something," there is still no umbrella organization in the United States coordinating the activities of individuals working to help Syrian Jews. The Anti-Defamation League sends a Syrian Jew to a conference in Rome on reparations for Libyan Jews. George Gruen of the American Jewish Committee publishes an article from time to time. Response from Reform congregations to the UAHC fact sheet on Syrian Jews has been negligible. And a spokesman with the National Jewish Community Relations Council, the group that circulated the fact sheet, counsels doing little publicly at this time because "Syrian Jews who really want to leave can do so if they leave their property, go through the hills, and smuggle themselves out to Turkey."[1] The same "authority" suggests working with WO-JAC (World Organization of Jews from Arab Countries). Only there is no WO-JAC. Following its much ballyhooed conference in Washington, D.C. late in 1987, WOJAC, like General Clay's Committee of Concern before it, disintegrated and is currently being reconstituted as a one-man operation. That one man, incidentally, has suggested that Jews in Syria are somewhat comfortable today, no worse than Arabs in Israel.

The facts are otherwise. According to my sources, fear is strong among Syria's Jews—fear of a resumption of restrictions by the government at any time, fear of Palestinians, of adult Palestinians who have beaten Jewish children at Purim and other holidays, fear that in the event of another war, all will die. Recently, the officer in charge of the Jewish Section in the *Muhabarat* lost his wife in an auto accident and has clamped down on innocents. Six Jews remain imprisoned in the filthy Adra prison, bent over in tiny cells seventy feet below ground level. All have been tortured and one (an eighteen-year-old Laham boy) was beaten so badly that he suffered from phlebitis. His father, visiting the jail, pleaded with the *Muhabarat*, "Take me! Kill me instead!"[2] Amnesty International issued a second protest on the prisoners' behalf in December, 1988. But not even Amnesty could establish the whereabouts of the brothers Elie and Selim Swed, neither of whom has been seen in the past fourteen months. According to one source, "Their mother is sick. Their father died of a coronary brought on by the arrests. They have received no change of underwear and that can only mean one thing. If the brothers are alive, it would be a miracle."[3]

The Assad government continues to promote international terrorism. As host to Ahmed Jibril's Popular Front for the Liberation of Palestine, General Command, Syria has been implicated, along with Libya, in the December, 1988 bombing of Pan-Am Flight 103 from London. The murder of 270 persons in an instant may be difficult to grasp, but the suffering of a single child is something else. Every day, a nine-year-old Syrian Jewish boy, living in the United States, is taken by his father to Sloan-Kettering Medical Center in New York City. He has no hair, his face is yellow. He is undergoing chemotherapy. He has cancer of the right eye and he is dying. Every day, his father weeps, because the mother and two other children (aged seven and four) are back in Syria, unable to leave the country.

An American student bicycles through the Middle East and publishes an article in *Israel Focus*, stating how things are pretty good for the "prosperous" Syrian-Jewish community. Misinformed volunteers working with American federations fret about jeopardizing the lives of Jews in Damascus. Yet the unanimous cry from those who know the truth (the Israeli Foreign Ministry, Judy Feld Carr and her Canadian Comittee, Dr. Gruen, the refugees in Gilo and Brooklyn, Syrian-Jewish college youth in the United States, those still trapped in Syria, even U.S. consular officials in the Middle East) is for public agitation, pressing Syria to honor basic human rights.

Notes

Preface

1. American Jewish Committee Involvement in European Protest on Behalf of Lebanese and Syrian Jews," memorandum, American Jewish Committee, March 1986, p. 2.
2. Honey and Irving Milstein, report, National Committee for Jews in Arab Lands, Toronto, April 11, 1977, p. 1.
3. Interview with Arlette Adler, Haifa, April 3, 1986.

Chapter 1: The Myth of Islamic Toleration

1. The argument that a Semitic fraternity existed in the Middle East until the rise of modern, political Zionism has been embraced by major scholars such as Sydney Fisher (*The Middle East: A History*, New York: Knopf, 1959), William Yale (*The Near East: A Modern History*, Ann Arbor: University of Michigan, 1958), Don Peretz (*The Middle East*, Boston: Houghton-Mifflin, 1969), and Yahya Armajani and Thomas Ricks (*The Middle East, Past and Present*, Englewood Cliffs, N.J.: Prentice Hall, 1970). See also the partisan works of Hisham Sharabi, Philip Hitti, Fred Khouri, Maxime Rodinson, George Kirk, Anthony Nutting, Sir John Baggot Glubb, and Edward Said. For a different view, consult Andre Chouraqui, *Between East and West: A History of Jews of North Africa* (Philadelphia: Jewish Publication Society of America, 1968); Bernard Lewis, *Semites and Anti-Semites* (New York: Norton, 1986); Albert Memmi, *Jews and Arabs*, trans. by Eleanor Levieux (Chicago: O'Hara, 1975); Hayyim Cohen, *The Jews of the Middle East, 1860–1972* (Jerusalem: Israel Universities Press, 1973); and Joan Peters, *From Time Immemorial: The Origins of the Arab-Jewish Conflict Over Palestine* (New York: Harper & Row, 1984).

2. Muslims insist that translations do no justice to the poetry and nuances of the Quran. Readers may consult the flowery English version of Mohammed Marmaduke Pickthall (*The Meaning of the Glorious Koran*, New York: Mentor, 1953). All of my citations, however, have come from N. J. Dawood, *The Koran* (Harmondsworth, U.K.: Penguin, 1956).

3. D. F. Green, ed., *Arab Theologians on Jews and Israel*, fourth Conference of the Academy of Islamic Research, al-Azhar, Cairo (Geneva: Editions de l'Avenir, 1971), p. 45.

4. Bat Ye'or, *Dhimmi Peoples: Oppressed Nations* (Geneva: Editions de l'Avenir, 1978).

5. Saul S. Friedman, "The Myth of Arab Toleration," *Midstream* 16 (January 1970):57.

6. According to Maurice Roumani, "the eighteenth-century Egyptian lords Ali Bey and Qaid Bey extorted huge sums in gold causing complete financial ruin" to their Jewish subjects. Jews in Iraq and Morocco also suffered from heavy taxes. *The Case of the Jews from Arab Countries: A Neglected Issue* (Tel Aviv: World Organization of Jews from Arab Countries, 1977), p. 27.

7. Saul S. Friedman, *Land of Dust: Palestine at the Turn of the Century* (Washington: University Press of America, 1982), p. 136.

8. Joseph B. Schechtman, *On Wings of Eagles: The Plight, Exodus, and Homecoming of Oriental Jewry* (New York and London: T. Yoseloff, 1961), pp. 40–41. Schechtman's book is essential for an understanding of the Jewish experience in Muslim countries.

9. S. D. Goitein, *Jews and Arabs: Their Contacts through the Ages* (reprint, New York: Schocken, 1974), pp. 73–74.

10. Heinrich Graetz, *History of the Jews* (1894; reprint, Philadelphia: Jewish Publication Society of America, 1956) Vol. III, pp. 75–82, 85, 119, 145, 163, 176–77, 201, 213, 247, 255, 278–79, 338, 347, 358, 361, 383, 387, 428, 454, 463, and 649; Vol. IV, pp. 389, 396, 553, 594, and 633. See also Walter Fischel, *Jews in the Economic and Political Life of Medieval Islam* (New York: Ktav, 1969); Jacob Marcus, *The Medieval World: A Source Book* (Philadelphia: Jewish Publication Society of America, 1960); and Goitein, *Jews and Arabs*, p. 67.

11. Goitein argues (*Jews and Arabs*, pp. 74–75) that this separation has a long history and should not be compared at all with the ghetto of European Jews. Yet he refers to the condition as hateful, originating in religious persecution.

12. Schechtman offers a depressing assessment of North African mellahs, in which population densities were three or four times the worst Muslim quarters and the people (35 percent of them dependent on charity) were infested with ringworm and trachoma. *On Wings of Eagles*, pp. 273–78. See also Nathan Ausubel, *A Pictorial History of the Jewish People* (New York: Crown, 1965), pp. 223–28.

13. For the grottos of Libya, see Schechtman, *On Wings of Eagles*, p. 128. For the cliff dwellers of the Atlas Mountains, see Ausubel, *A Pictoral History*, pp. 225–27.

14. For al-Hakim, see P. M. Holt, Ann Lambton, and Bernard Lewis, eds., *Cambridge History of Islam* (Cambridge: Cambridge University Press, 1970), Vol. I, pp. 186–88; Philip Hitti, *History of the Arabs* (reprint, New York: St. Martin's Press, 1968), pp. 620–21; and Bernard Lewis, *Islam* (New York: Harper Torch, 1974) Vol. I, pp. 46–59.

15. Cecil Roth, "Jews in the Arab World," *Near East Report: Myths and Facts* (special survey, August 1967):B–17–20.

16. Graetz, *History of the Jews*, Vol. III, passim.

17. Schechtman, *On Wings of Eagles*, pp. 35–38 and Itzhak Ben-Zvi, *The Exiled and the Redeemed* (Philadelphia: Jewish Publication Society of America, 1957), pp. 23–31 and 207–208.

18. Graetz, *History of the Jews*, Vol. III, pp. 321–43.

19. Bat Ye'or, *The Dhimmi: Jews and Christians under Islam*, trans. by David Maisel, Paul Fenton, and David Littman (London and New York: Farleigh Dickinson, 1985), p. 87.

20. Norman Stillman, *The Jews of Arab Lands* (Philadelphia: Jewish Publication Society of America, 1979), p. 84. See also Ye'or, *The Dhimmi*, pp. 143 and 292.

21. Brandeis Professor Alfred Ivry, statement, *Canadian Jewish News* (March 26, 1987).

22. Bat Ye'or, *The Dhimmi*, p. 72. Goitein waffles on the subject of the poll tax, arguing that it sometimes was a benefit designed to "safeguard" the life and property of "a protected person." Goitein states that "when the known facts are weighed, I believe it is correct to say that as a whole the position of the non-Muslims under Arab Islam was far better than that of the Jews in Medieval Christian Europe" (*Jews and Arabs*, p. 84). Four pages later, he closes the same chapter by writing, "The moving plaints of the great Hebrew poet Yehuda Halevi (d. 1141) who had lived both in Muslim and in Christian Spain, that the one was as bad as the other is an eloquent testimony to this state of affairs" (*Jews and Arabs*, p. 88).

23. L. S. Stavrianos, *The Ottoman Empire* (New York: Holt, Rinehart and Winston, 1957), p. 33.

24. Edward Lane, quoted in David Littman and Bat Ye'or, *Protected Peoples under Islam* (Geneva: Centre d'Information et de Documentation sur le Moyen-Orient, 1976), p. 12.

25. Ahmed Rihani, quoted in Schechtman, *On Wings of Eagles*, p. 42.

26. Neville Mandel, "Turks, Arabs and Jewish Immigration into Palestine, 1882–1914," in *Middle East Affairs*, Vol. 4, Albert Hourani, ed. (London: Oxford, 1965), pp. 84–85.

27. Littman and Ye'or, *Protected Peoples*, pp. 6–7.

28. Roumani, *The Case of the Jews*, pp. 23–24.

29. Bernard Lewis, "The Pro-Islamic Jews," *Judaism* 17(4) (1968):401.

30. Goitein, *Jews and Arabs*, p. 76.

31. Lewis, "The Pro-Islamic Jews," p. 401.

Chapter 2: Arab-Jewish Relations in the Twentieth Century

1. A short list of works on the conflicting claims for Palestine might include George Antonius, *The Arab Awakening* (New York: G. P. Putnam, 1946); Ben Halpern, *The Idea of a Jewish State* (Cambridge, Mass.: Harvard, 1961); J. C. Hurewitz, *The Struggle for Palestine* (New York: Norton, 1950); Url Ranaan, *Frontiers of a Nation* (Westport, Conn.: Hyperion Press, 1975); Howard Sachar, *A History of Israel* (New York: Knopf, 1976); Leonard Stein, *The Balfour Declaration* (London, 1961); and Esco Foundation for Palestine, *Palestine: A Study of Jewish, Arab, and British Policies* (New Haven, Conn.: Yale, 1947).

2. On the life and work of the Grand Mufti, see Aharon Cohen, *Israel and the Arab World* (New York: Funk and Wagnalls, 1970); Norman Bentwich, *Mandate Memories, 1918–1948* (New York: Schocken, 1965); Yehoshva Porath, *The Emergence of the Pal-*

estinian Arab National Movement, 1918–1929 (London: Frank Cass, 1974); Howard Sachar, *The Emergence of the Middle East, 1914–1924* (New York: Knopf, 1969), pp. 392–407; Howard Sachar, *Europe Leaves the Middle East, 1936–1954* (New York: Knopf, 1972); William Ziff, *The Rape of Palestine* (New York and Toronto: Longmans, Green & Co., 1938); Lukasz Hirszowicz, *The Third Reich and the Arab East* (London and Toronto: University of Toronto Press, 1966); and Joseph Schechtman, *The Mufti and the Fuehrer* (New York and London: T. Yoseloff, 1965).

3. According to Dieter Wisliceny, "He (the mufti) was one of Eichmann's best friends and had constantly incited him to accelerate the extermination measures. I heard him say that accompanied by Eichmann, he had visited incognito the gas chamber of Auschwitz," cited in Schechtman, *The Mufti and the Fuehrer*, p. 160. Nazi-hunter Simon Wiesenthal claims the mufti lavished praise on Rudolf Hess, commandant of Auschwitz, Franz Ziereis of Mauthausen, Dr. Siegfried Seidl of Theresienstadt, and Josef Kramer of Bergen-Belsen. Simon Wiesenthal, *Grossmufti—Grossagent der Achse* (Salzburg, 1947), pp. 51, 53, and 54.

4. Elias Cooper, "Forgotten Palestinian: The Nazi Mufti," *American Zionist* 68 (special issue, March-April 1978):15.

5. Schechtman, *The Mufti and the Fuehrer*, p. 162. Cooper claims the mufti had access to documents relevant to the final solution in Buro IVAb, "Forgotten Palestinian," p. 28.

6. Cited in Howard Sachar, *The Course of Modern Jewish History* (Cleveland: World Publishing, 1958), p. 461. See also John Bagot Glubb, *A Soldier with the Arabs* (New York: Harper & Bros., 1958).

7. Arafat said, "While we were vociferously condemning the massacres of Jews under Nazi rule, Zionist leadership appeared more interested at that time in exploiting them as best it could in order to realize its goal of immigration to Palestine." *Palestine Lives: Address by Mr. Yasser Arafat, November 13, 1974*, (Washington, D.C.: Free Palestine) pp. 19–20.

8. Saul S. Friedman, "Arab Complicity in the Holocaust," *Jewish Frontier* 42 (April 1975):10. See also Friedman, *No Haven for the Oppressed: United States Policy Toward Jewish Refugees, 1938–1945* (Detroit: Wayne State, 1973), pp. 155–180 and 198–99.

9. Martin Gilbert, *The Jews of Arab Lands: Their History in Maps* (London: Board of Deputies of British Jews, 1976), pp. 5 and 8.

10. Of the Libyan pogroms, Clifton Daniel reported that babies were beaten to death with iron bars, old men hacked to pieces, and expectant mothers disemboweled. Cited in Joseph B. Schechtman, *On Wings of Eagles: The Plight, Exodus, and Homecoming of Oriental Jewry* (New York and London: T. Yoseloff, 1961), p. 134. For the massacres in Iraq, see pp. 97–98; Aden, pp. 78–79; Syria, pp. 154–55; and Egypt, pp. 187–88.

11. Ibid., 92–95, 102–103, and 131–32.

12. *New York Times*, Jan. 27, 1969, p. 1.

13. Dr. Susan Hattis-Rolef, ed., *Freedom of Trade and the Arab Boycott* (New York: Anti-Defamation League, 1985).

14. Schechtman, *On Wings of Eagles*, pp. 79, 105–106, 116–23, 135, 162–63, and 204.

15. Yehuda Dominitz, "Immigration and Absorption of Jews from Arab Countries," summary report, for the World Organization of Jews from Arab Countries Conference, Washington, October 1987, pp. 1–6.

16. The American Joint Distribution Committee, *1985–1986 Annual Report*, p. 31.

See also Wendy Elliman, "Jews in Arab Lands Today," *Focus* (British/Israel Public Affairs Committee, April 1986) and George Gruen, "The Forgotten Victims of the Arab-Israel Conflict," memorandum, American Jewish Committee, June 7, 1987.

17. All statistics taken from *Statistical Yearbook, United Nations, 1981* and George Thomas Kurian, ed., *Encyclopedia of the Third World: Facts on File* (New York: Facts on File, Inc., 1982).

18. "Situation of Jews in the Middle East and North Africa," report, American Jewish Committee, 1972, pp. 19–25.

19. George Gruen, "Morocco: Plotting for Peace?" *Reform Judaism* 28 (June 1981):10–11.

20. The Joint Distribution Committee registered concern about the growing militance, *Annual Report*, p. 15. See also George Gruen, "Tunisia's Troubled Jewish Community," report, American Jewish Committee, November 15, 1983.

21. Goitein maintains that "the entire Jewish population" of Yemen was miraculously transferred by air to Israel. *Jews and Arabs: Their Contacts through the Ages* (New York: Schocken, 1974), p. 203.

22. Yemenis have a different view of relations with Jews. According to one local source, Muslim women often visited Jewish women to learn certain skills from them. They people sang together and any Muslim who wronged a Jew would be fined or imprisoned. "Jews, especially the elders, were known to be truthful. They would mind their own business (were quiet, etc.) but would not by any means tolerate insults or any wrongs committed against them." When Jews of the al-Nadirah district were informed that they were being permitted to leave Yemen, in fulfillment of the Biblical prophecy, Muslims and Jews wept. A great feast was held in honor of the departing community and a Jewish butcher was put in charge of preparing the meat. "The Jews refused to ride on donkeys when departing, so that they could leave their tears in the dust on the road to Aden" (A. Alhadi, report [Youngstown: unpublished, September 1986]).

23. "Situation of the Jews in the Middle East and North Africa," report, American Jewish Committee, 1972, Section V. p. 17.

24. George Gruen, "The Murder of Lebanese Jewish Hostages," report, American Jewish Committee, January 17, 1986 and "Lebanese Jews—Victims of Shiite Muslim Terror," report, American Jewish Committee, February 20, 1986. Rachel Hallak, a widow of one of the victims, submitted a poignant letter to *Le Monde* in March, 1986 telling how her husband had been abducted. Cited in "Lebanon's Jewish Hostages: What Next?" American Jewish Committe, July 7, 1988.

25. Sheldon Kirshner, "Lebanon: Strife Devastates Jewish Community," report, Canadian Jewish Congress, Committee for Jews in Arab Lands, Ontario, May–June, 1985, p. 1.

26. Based on personal observations made while visiting Cairo during Passover 1986, one week after the United States' raid against Libya.

27. Joint Distribution Committee, *Annual Report*, p. 15.

28. George Gruen, "Current Situation of Jews in Arab Lands," report, American Jewish Committee, October 23, 1973, pp. 2–3.

29. Nick Thimmesch, "Inside Baghdad," *New York Jewish Week* (March 4, 1983).

30. "Iraqis Too Busy with War to Hassle Nation's Jews," *New York Jewish Week* (March 4, 1983).

31. Louis Gottesman, "Iranian Jewry: Since the Revolution," *News and Views* 4 (American Jewish Committee, Spring 1982):32 B–C; "Details on Reports of Iranian

Execution of Seventh Jew," American Jewish Committee, report, December 22, 1980; and George Gruen, "Iranian Jewry and the Execution of Albert Danielpour," background memorandum, American Jewish Committee Foreign Affairs, June 11, 1980.

32. Letter to author from Dr. Gruen, November 18, 1986.

33. George Gruen, "Schizophrenic Turkey," *Present Tense* 9 (Autumn 1981):47–50.

34. On Turkey, see George Gruen, "Turkey's Relations with Israel and Its Arab Neighbors," *Middle East Review* 17 (Spring 1985):33–43; "Combating Terrorism: Lessons from the Istanbul Massacre," memorandum, American Jewish Committee, October 14, 1986; "Turkey after the Military Coup: Impact on the Jewish Community and on Turkish-Israel Relations," report, American Jewish Committee, March 26, 1981; and "JDC Eyewitness Account of Funeral for Istanbul Murder Victims," reports from the field, September 19, 1986. Dr. Gruen also prepared an excellent update on the current status of Jews in the Islamic world, "The Other Refugees: Impact of Nationalism, Anti-Zionism and the Arab-Israel Conflict on the Jews of the Arab World," the World Organization of Jews from Arab Countries, conference in Washington, D.C., October 1987.

35. See Lois Gottesman, "Jews in the Middle East," *American Jewish Yearbook* 75 (1985):304–310.

Chapter 3: A Humanitarian Gesture

1. *New York Times*, Jan. 5, 1984, sect. A, p. 14.

2. *New York Times*, Dec. 30, 1983, sect. A, p. 8.

3. *New York Times*, Dec. 6, 1983, sect. A, p. 1.

4. *New York Times*, Jan. 1, 1984, p. 8 and Jan. 5, 1984, sect. A, p. 14.

5. *New York Times*, Dec. 26, 1983.

6. *New York Times*, Dec. 6, 1983, p. 1.

7. *New York Times*, Dec. 30, 1983, p. 22 and Jan. 4, 1984, p. 18.

8. *New York Times*, Jan. 4, 1983.

9. *Newsweek* 103 (January 9, 1984):20–21 and (January 16, 1984):14–15.

10. *U.S. News and World Report* talked of Jackson "cutting a wide swatch," 96 (January 16, 1984):5 and 22. *Time* tempered its enthusaism, labeling Jackson's feat "dubious diplomacy," 123 (January 9, 1984): 21 and "historical theater," Ibid., 10–14.

11. *New York Times*, Jan. 5, 1984, sect. A, p. 14.

12. "The Syrian Connection: A Multi-Dimensional Threat." *ADL Bulletin*, 44 (April 1987):12–13.

13. *New York Times*, Feb. 23, 1984, sect. B, p. 13.

14. *New York Times*, Feb. 26, 1984, sect. A, p. 29.

15. *New York Times*, Apr. 10, 1984, sect. B, p. 8.

16. *New York Times*, Feb. 23, 1984, sect. A, p. 20.

17. Report, American Jewish Committee, January 11, 1984 and Judy Feld Carr, Schermer Scholar-in-Residence Lecture, Youngstown State University, January 24, 1985.

18. *Le Monde* (November 10, 1984):2. Author's translation.

19. Interview with Israel Foreign Office, Jerusalem, May 20, 1986.

20. Interview with Rabbi Isaac F., Deal, N.J., September 21, 1986.

21. Interview with Steve Shalom, New York City, September 23, 1986.

22. Interview with Moishe Cohen, the World Organization of Jews from Arab Countries, Tel Aviv, May 15, 1986.

23. "Jews in Arab Lands," *CJC Bulletin* (May 1984):1.

24. *Department of State Bulletins* 84 (1984):8. Statements by Kenneth Dam, Feb., 1984, pp. 27–28; George Schultz, March, 1984, p. 35; and Lawrence Eagleburger, March, 1984, p. 51.

25. "A Troubled Minority," reprinted *Newsweeek* article in American Jewish Committee report, undated.

26. Undated memorandum, Israel Foreign Office, p. 1.

27. Joseph B. Schechtman, *On Wings of Eagles: The Plight, Exodus, and Homecoming of Oriental Jewry* (New York and London: T. Yoseloff, 1961), p. 150–51.

28. Ibid., 154.

29. David Sitton, *Sephardi Communities Today* (Jerusalem: Council of Sephardi and Oriental Communities, 1985), p. 73.

30. Schechtman, *On Wings of Eagles*, pp. 154–62.

31. Ibid., 162.

32. Bartley Crum, *Behind the Silken Curtain: A Personal Account of Anglo-American Diplomacy in Palestine and the Middle East* (New York: Simon and Schuster, 1947), p. 239.

33. Anne Sinai and Allen Pollack, eds., *The Syrian Arab Republic* (New York: American Professors for Peace in the Middle East, 1976), p. 170.

34. Saul S. Friedman, "The Anguish of Syrian Jewry," *Midstream* 21 (June-July 1975):16.

35. Dr. Heskel Haddad, "The Jewish Refugees from Arab Countries," *APPME Middle East Information Series* 16 (November 1971):29–33.

36. *La haine est sacrée* (Jerusalem: Academic Press, 1968), p. 6.

37. Ibid. 19.

38. The government listed Jewish businesses on Shuhada, Hunya, el-Kasa, and el-Suf streets. *Plight of Syrian Jewry*, compiled by International Conference for Deliverance of the Jews in the Middle East (Paris, 1974), pp. 15–17.

39. Statement on Jews in Syria," report, Committee of Concern, October 7, 1971. The report also mentioned Jewish girls who had been abducted, raped, and thrown naked into the streets of the Damascus ghetto. See also National Committee for Jews in Arab Lands, *Fact Sheet: Jews in Syria*, Canadian Jewish Congress, Toronto, 1972.

40. Jewish Telegraph Agency, November 19, 1971.

41. Pierre Demeron, "An Uncommon Aspect of Syria, The Damascus Jews," *La Tribune des Nations* (May 7, 1971):6–13.

42. Ibid., 7.

43. Ibid., 8.

44. Ibid., 8.

45. Ibid., 12–13.

46. Ibid., 13.

47. *New York Times*, Jan. 5, 1975, p. 18.

48. Mike Wallace, "At Large," CBS Radio, February 4, 1974.

49. Sinai and Pollack, *Syrian Arab Republic*, p. 69.

50. Robert Azzi, "Damascus: Syria's Uneasy Eden," *National Geographic* 145 (April 1974):512–35.

51. For Edward Gilbert Grosvenor's retraction see *National Geographic* 145 (November 1974):587.

52. Judy Siegel, "The Nightmare of Syrian Jews," *Jerusalem Post*, Apr. 19, 1974.

128   NOTES

Chapter 4: The Deal Debating Society

1. Deal ranks with such exclusive suburbs as Greenwich, Connecticut, Mill Neck, New York, and Atherton, California. *Cleveland Plain Dealer*, Sept. 9, 1987, sect. A, p. 12. Background on the town came from interviews with David Richard, Jack Rothnemer, and Mrs. I. Shama in Deal, September 20–21, 1986.

2. For the most comprehensive telling of the story of Syrian Jews in the United States, see Joseph Sutton, *Magic Carpet: Aleppo in Flatbush* (New York: Thayer-Jacoby, 1979) and *Aleppo Chronicles* (New York: Thayer-Jacoby, 1987).

3. The scene was reconstructed from discussions held in a Deal synagogue on Saturday afternoon, September 20, 1986.

4. *Amnesty International Report 1983* (London, 1983), pp. 328–30. Ironically, the report cites six pages of Israeli violations, pp. 311–16. For additional verification of Syrian torture, see Mordechai Nisan, *Human Rights in the Arab Countries* (New York: APPME, 1981).

5. Interview with Rabbi Isaac F., Deal, September 21, 1986.

6. Lynn Simarski, "The Lure of Aleppo," *Aramco World* 38 (July-August 1987):34–41.

7. Before the so-called civil war erupted in Lebanon in 1974 the border with Syria was practically open to tens of thousands of Syrian Christians or Muslims who passed with little difficulty.

8. It seemed logical to assume the boys would make for the Turkish border, which was only 50 miles north of Aleppo. The road to Lebanon lay more than 100 miles to the south through the provinces of Idlib, Hama, and Homs.

9. *Sochnut* is another name for the Jewish Agency in Israel. Once a kind of shadow government of the World Zionist Organization in Palestine, it relinquished most of its functions to the newly formed state in 1948. The *Sochnut* helped assimilate 239,000 immigrants in 1949 and continues to assist people making *aliyah* to Israel. Its Education and Culture Department operates *ulpanim* (language seminars) and supplies rabbis, cantors, and instructors to kibbutzim. The Agriculture Department may be its biggest employer (1,500 people) and spender ($50 million per year). Ernest Strock, "Jewish Agency," in *Encyclopedia Judaica*, Vol. 10 (Jerusalem: Keter, 1971), pp. 26–35.

Chapter 5: Sophie's Choice

1. Interview with Mr. Gross, Williamsburg, September 22, 1986.

2. This charismatic sect of Chasidic Judaism was established by a Galician leader in Satu Mare, Hungary, at the end of the eighteenth century. In 1947, Joel Teitelbaum transferred the seat of his dynasty to Brooklyn. At one time, he was also considered the spiritual leader of the fundamentalist Neturei Karta group in Jerusalem. The Satmarers oppose Zionism for alleged *halakhic* reasons. A Jewish state must not exist before the coming of the messiah. The use of Hebrew in the vernacular should be forbidden. Furthermore, the Holocaust is deemed a divine punishment for the sins of the Jewish people. See Avraham Rubinstein, "Teitelbaum," in *Encyclopedia Judaica*, Vol. 15 (Jerusalem: Keter, 1971), pp. 908–10.

3. Interview with Mrs. Gamaliel, September 22, 1986. See also seven-page statement offered to the Canadian Jewish Congress Plenary, May 8, 1986.

4. It was standard procedure to tie people, with head down, inside a truck tire and

shock them with cattle prods. See Yosef Alfer, *The Story of Israeli Prisoners in Syria*, edited and translated by Pamela Fitton (Jerusalem: Keter Books, 1969); International Conference for the Deliverance of the Jews in the Middle East, *Plight of Syrian Jewry* (Paris, 1974), pp. 25–28; and Committee for Jewry in Foreign Lands, "Report," *Beth Tzedec Bulletin* (Toronto, September 25, 1974), p. 1.

5. A *golem* literally was an incomplete thing or shapeless mass. Jewish tradition, like that of Roman and English Gothic literature, redounds with tales of creatures produced by supernatural means. The most famous *golem*, a guardian of the Prague ghetto, was formed of the "four prime elements" by Rabbi Judah Loew in the sixteenth century.

6. New York Association of New Americans (NYANA) is a social work agency that is derivative of HIAS-HICEM, earlier self-help organizations that assisted Jewish immigrants and refugees in adapting to the United States and Canada.

7. Interview with Mrs. C., NYANA, and Judy Feld Carr, December 19, 1986.

8. Interview with Judy Feld Carr, September 26, 1986. Mrs. Carr subsequently arranged for the Gamaliels to obtain a videocassette recorder to help Mr. Gamaliel learn English. On visiting the family recently she noticed that someone, obviously a fundamentalist Satmarer who opposes the use of television, had scrawled on the wall outside the apartment, "The devil lives here." Interview, August 24, 1987.

9. Interview with Sepharic *Bikur Holim*, September 24, 1986. The work of this agency is fully outlined in its *Bulletin*, March 1986.

Chapter 6: Freedom to Emigrate

1. S. D. Goitein, *Jews and Arabs: Their Contacts through the Ages* (reprint, New York: Schocken, 1974) p. 76. Jews who managed to leave a country forfeited their property.

2. Universal Declaration of the Rights of Man, adopted by the United Nations on December 5, 1948, cited in Louis Snyder, *The Making of Modern Man* (Princeton: D. Van Nostrand, 1967), pp. 739–40.

3. Interview with Judy Feld Carr, November 30, 1986.

4. George Gruen, "Update on Jews in Arab Lands," report, American Jewish Committee, May 8, 1987, p. 2.

5. The following account comes from *Syria: A Prison to 4500 Jews: Reports of Beth Tzedec Bulletin and Committee for Jews in Arab Lands* (Canadian Jewish Congress, Toronto, September 4, 1974) and interviews with Judy Feld Carr, February 14–16, 1975.

6. Author's telephone conversation with Judy Feld Carr, February 12, 1975.

7. Interview with Judy Feld Carr, January 25, 1985.

8. *New York Times*, Apr. 14, 1974, p. 2.

9. Interview with Mr. Elias, September 25, 1986, Brooklyn.

10. Material for the Zeibak affair was amassed from correspondence with Judy Feld Carr; Isaiah Terman, "Trial of Syrian Jews Resumes in Damascus," report, American Jewish Committee, n.d.; A. A. Rosen, Director of the American Defense League Chicago office, "Trial of Syrian Jews," memorandum, July 8, 1974; Committee of Concern on Murder of Jewish Women in Syria, statement, March 25, 1974; letter, Robert F. Leonard, District Attorneys Association, August 20, 1974; Livio Caputo, "We Spoke to Jews Who Must Live in Syria," *Epoca* (April 28, 1974) trans. by Canadian Committee for Arab Jews; telephone interview with Dr. George Gruen, Director of Middle East Affairs, American Jewish Committee, February 3, 1975.

11. *Le Figaro*, March 9, 1974, "Quatre femmes juives assassiness à Damas," reproduced in *Plight of Syrian Jewry* (Paris: International Conference for Deliverance of Jews in the Middle East, 1974), p. 33.

12. Livio Caputo, "Drama in the Ghetto of Damascus," in *Plight of Syrian Jewry*, p. 39.

13. Committee of Concern, statement, March 26, 1974.

14. Author's telephone interviews with George Gruen and Judy Feld Carr, February 3, 1975.

15. Caputo, "Drama in the Ghetto of Damascus," p. 41.

16. Ibid., 40.

17. *New York Times*, May 14, 1974, p. 3.

18. There is no indication in Nixon's memoirs that he did this. See Richard Nixon, *The Memoirs of Richard Nixon* (New York: Grosset and Dunlap, 1978) and William Safire, *Before the Fall* (Garden City, N.J.: Doubleday, 1975).

19. Interview with George Gruen, February 3, 1975.

20. Dr. Ada Aharoni wrote *Four Jewish Syrian Daughters*. Born in Cairo, she emigrated to Israel in 1950. A professor of literature and history at the Technion, Haifa, Dr. Aharoni has published ten books. The poem is taken from "Let Them Go! Syrian Jewry in Distress," a leaflet published by the Israel Council for the Rescue of Jews in Arab Countries, Tel Aviv.

Chapter 7: The Bahats

1. On Leo Baeck as "a witness of faith," see Akiba Ernst Simon, "Leo Baeck," *Encyclopedia Judaica*, Vol. 4 (Jerusalem: Keter, 1971), p. 78.

2. Rabbi Irving Rosenbaum, *The Holocaust and Halakhah* (New York: Ktav, 1976), pp. 23–24. I am indebted to Rabbi Mitchell Kornspan of Youngstown for this *teshuvah*.

3. Interview with Rabbi Yehudah, Brooklyn, September 25, 1986.

4. Interview with Moishe Cohen, Tel Aviv, May 15, 1986.

5. Joseph B. Schechtman, *On Wings of Eagles: The Plight, Exodus, and Homecoming of Oriental Jewry* (New York and London: T. Yoseloff, 1961), p. 160.

6. In a discussion with a Haifa University professor (May 29, 1986), the question came up why Jews remained. The educator, showing little empathy remarked, "The Syrian Jews had the opportunity to leave. Some did. The majority did. Those who didn't, I don't know why they didn't."

7. In 1971, an Iranian Jew attending Youngstown State University enrolled in my Holocaust seminar. In subsequent discussions, Fahri M. expressed harsh criticism of German Jews who failed to appreciate dangers posed by Hitler and the Nazis. When asked what he might do in a similar situation, he replied, "That kind of thing will never happen in Iran."

8. Interview with Shulamit Bahat, Tel Kabir, March 23, 1986.

9. Interview with Simcha Bahat, Tel Kabir, March 23, 1986.

10. Interview with spokesman of Canadian Committee for Jews in Arab Lands, Toronto, February 1984.

11. Ibid.

12. Ibid.

13. Interviews with the Bahats, March 23, 1986.

Chapter 8: Purim 1986

1. In 1970, the Youngstown Zionist District underwrote a campus organization at Youngstown State University to provide social and political activity for Jewish students. When its first public meeting in December ended in a near free-for-all with Arab demonstrators, James R., a local philanthropist, scored the officers of the organization, some of whom were Persian Jews, offering these insights.

2. Literally "one hundred gates," Mea Shearim was the first Jewish settlement outside the walls of the Old City of Jerusalem. Created by religious pilgrims at the end of the nineteenth century, it is a center of extreme fundamentalism. Ironically, the Neturei Karta Chasidic sect located here does not even recognize the state of Israel.

3. Adherents of the motto "The Land of Israel for the people of Israel according to the Torah of Israel." The *Mizrachi* movement was founded by such rabbis as Shmuel Moghilever, Mair (Berlin) Bar-Ilan, and Isaac Reines. Although a distinct minority in Israel, it wields substantial influence through banks, settlements, and its National Religious party. See Louis Bernstein, "Mizrachi," *Encyclopedia Judaica*, Vol. 12 (Jerusalem: Keter, 1976), pp. 175–180.

4. Interview with the Hadli brothers, Tel Aviv, March 22, 1986.

5. Another teenager testified to the severity of such crackdowns. *Syrian Jewry in Distress* (Israel Council for Rescue of Jews in Arab Countries, n.d.), p. 28.

6. "Syria: A Prison to 4500 Jews," report, Beth Tzedec Rescue Committee, February 20, 1974.

7. *Syrian Jewry in Distress* offers the testimony of a man who, fleeing Syria with his wife and four children, likened himself to Amos on the day of judgment, p. 30.

8. For Mr. Nuseyri, see *Syrian Jewry in Distress*, chapter 3, notes 47 and 48.

9. Author's telephone interview with Judy Feld Carr, July 10, 1986.

Chapter 9: Abu Wujjah, Father of Pain

1. For a stirring refutation of many atrocity charges, see "Torturing the Truth," *The New Republic* editorial, 180 (February 24, 1979):5–8.

2. In 1987, the free world was shocked when a pro-Palestinian group calling itself Law in the Service of Man charged that youths in Gaza had been systematically tortured by Israeli troops. Some reportedly had their heads rammed into walls, cigarettes applied to their ears, and hot eggs to their armpits. An Israeli military spokesman dismissed the accusations as "nonsense." *Cleveland Plain Dealer*, Aug. 6, 1987, sect. A, p. 9.

3. Six-page summary submitted by the government of Israel to the International Committee of the Red Cross, November 10, 1973.

4. *New York Times*, Feb. 4, 1972, p. 8 and Jan. 2, 1975, p. 5.

5. George Gruen, "Syrian Jews Face Perilous Future," report, American Jewish Committee, April 21, 1981, p. 1.

6. "Plight of Syrian Jewry" (report, Committee for Jewry in Foreign Lands and Beth Tzedec, September 25, 1974, pp. 25–28.

7. Amnesty International Reports (London, 1985), reprinted in Sara Averick, *A Human Rights Comparison: Israel Versus the Arab States* (Washington, D.C.: American-Israel Public Affairs Committee, 1988), p. 9.

8. All of the comments made by Yitzhak Tsur in this chapter were made during an interview in Jerusalem, April 11, 1986.

9. Shukri al-Kuwatli was a leader of the National Bloc, which eventually seized control of Syria during World War II. Named president in the first elections that were free of French control, he served from 1943 until Colonel Husni Zaim led a coup in March, 1949. Zaim was assassinated in August. Kuwatli returned to prominence with the Ba'athists after 1954 and engineered the short-lived union with Egypt's Nasser in 1958.

10. Elie Cohen was an Egyptian-born Jew who emigrated to Israel in 1957. An intelligence operative in Syria, he was exposed in January, 1965. The Syrian government denied him counsel, and despite interventions from leaders in France, Canada, and Belgium, as well as Pope Paul VI, they publicly executed Cohen in Damascus. See Y. Ben-Porat and U. Dan, *The Spy from Israel* (London: Valentine, Mitchell, 1969).

Chapter 10: A Death at the Door

1. Interview with Yaakov Khazzan, Tel Aviv, May 15, 1986.

2. All comments by Maurice Nissan in this chapter were made during an interview in Tel Kabir, March 21, 1986.

3. He means a fez.

4. Maurice Rouhani, *The Case of the Jews from Arab Countries* (Tel Aviv: World Organization of Jews from Arab Countries, 1977), p. 34.

5. David Sitton, *Sephardi Communities Today* (Jerusalem: Council of Sephardi and Oriental Communities, 1985), pp. 57–58.

6. Assad's mercurial brother Rifaat controlled the 20,000-man security force until the fall of 1985. Charges of corruption and a plot to overthrow the government sent him into temporary exile. *New York Times*, Oct. 31, 1985, sect. A, p. 6. A good assessment of the infighting of the Ba'athist government is provided by Kati Marton, "Peril or Possibility: America and Syria at the Crossroads," *Middle East Insight* 4 (1986): 11–25.

Chapter 11: Damascus: The Haret el-Yahud

1. Colin Thubron, *Mirror to Damascus* (Boston: Little, Brown, 1967), p. 147.

2. Ibid., 167.

3. Ibid.

4. Ibid.

5. Ibid.

6. Beth Tzedec Reports, Temple bulletins, Toronto, May 1 and 22, 1974.

7. Livio Caputo, "Drama in the Ghetto of Damascus," in *Plight of Syrian Jewry* (Paris: International Conference of Deliverance of Jews in the Middle East, 1974), p. 40.

8. "50th Anniversary Plenary," World Jewish Congress, January 29, 1985, p. 15. Unpublished report.

9. Interview with Steve Shalom, New York City, September, 23, 1986.

10. Interview with unnamed Syrian Jewish refugee, Tel Aviv, September 25, 1986.

11. Interview with Moishe Cohen, Tel Aviv, May 15, 1986.

12. Mitterand accomplished very little by his visit. According to the *New York Times*, he received a "stern, uncompromising statement" from Assad. See *New York Times*, Nov. 27, 1985, sect. I, p. 9 and Nov. 29, 1985, sect. I, p. 9.

13. The *Shemoneh Esreh* or eighteen benedictions constitute the heart of the Jewish

prayer service. Also known as the *Amidah* they are to be read while standing, as a form of reverence.

14. Interview with unnamed Syrian Jewish refugee, New York, September 25, 1986.

15. Interview with Mr. Elias, New York, September 25, 1986.

16. Interview with Benjamin Z., Deal, New Jersey, September 21, 1986.

17. Interview with Yaakov Khazzan, Tel Aviv, May 15, 1986.

Chapter 12: Qāmishlī

1. "The Euphrates Dam and Syrian-Iraqi Relations," in Anne Sinai and Allan Pollack, eds., *The Syrian Arab Republic* (New York: American Academic Assoc. for Peace in the Middle East, 1976), pp. 75–76.

2. The following comments were made during an interview with Albert and Orah Jamila, Gilo Absorption Center, April 11, 1986.

3. *Gadna* is an acronym for the Hebrew Youth Battalions' pre-military cadet corps in Israel.

4. Interview with Yosef Jamila, Gilo Absorption Center, May 7, 1986.

5. Interview with Rima Azur, Gilo Absorption Center, May 7, 1986.

6. Interview with Yosef Jamila, Gilo Absorption Center, May 7, 1986.

Chapter 13: Feminine Destiny

1. Herzlia's full story, "A Hunger Strike in the Women's Prison," is told in Yehuda Atlas, ed., *Ad Amud Hatlia* (Till the Hanging Tree) (Jerusalem: Ministry of Defense, 1969), pp. 201–08.

2. Interview with Herzlia Lokay, Haifa, May 27, 1986.

3. Interview with Moishe Cohen, Tel Aviv, May 15, 1986.

4. Edward Grossman, "Where the Melting Pot Failed," *Jerusalem Post Magazine* (May 30, 1986):8.

5. George Gruen, "Current Situation of Jews in Arab Lands," background memorandum, American Jewish Committee, October 23, 1973, p. 2.

6. Lokay interview, May 27, 1986.

7. Letter, Carol C. Laise, U.S. State Department to Lokay, April 5, 1974.

8. *New York Times*, Mar. 31, 1974, p. 9. Three years later, the U.N. secretary general, having accomplished little, promised Begin that he would intervene on behalf of 800 Jewish families. Again nothing substantive developed. *New York Times*, July 23, 1977, p. 2.

9. Letter, Charge d'Affairs Thomas Dunnigan to Lokay, May 9, 1977.

10. Statement of President Carter, *Department of State Bulletins* 77 (November 28, 1977):759.

11. *Department of State Bulletins* 76. See Christopher's statement to the subcommittee of the House Foreign Relations Committee, pp. 289–91, and statements by Vance on February 11 and 27, pp. 162–63 and 245.

12. Syria had been reported willing to end restrictions on Jews as early as December 29, 1976, *New York Times*, sect. I, p. 4. For Solarz's promising discussions after a month in the Middle East, see *New York Times*, Jan. 6, 1977, p. 3.

13. Carter saluted the leaders' "common backgrounds" and hailed the meeting as a "milestone to peace." *Department of State Bulletins*, 76 (May 9, 1977):595–96.

14. For Assad's cool response see *Department of State Bulletins* 76, p. 597.

15. Interview with Steve Shalom, New York, September 23, 1986. The *New York Times* offered two major articles (one dealing with the reaction of Sephardic synagogues in Brooklyn, the other replete with a map of Syria and a photograph of Selim Totah), July 31, 1977, sect. C, pp. 1 and 3.

16. Interview with Stella Farah, New York, September 24, 1986.

17. Interview with Jeanette Cattan, New York, September 24, 1986.

18. Farrah interview, September 24, 1986.

19. Shalom interview, September 23, 1986.

20. Interview with Sherry Hyman, Joint Distribution Committee, New York, September 23, 1986.

21. Lokay interview, May 27, 1986.

22. Ibid.

Chapter 14: Conclusion

1. *London Times*, Dec. 1, 1983, p. 8.

2. Laura Veltman, "Hostages in Syria," *Australian Jewish News*, (August 14, 1987):32.

3. Interview with Steve Shalom, New York, September 23, 1986.

4. Veltman, "Hostages in Syria," p. 31.

5. Interview with Rabbi Isaac Dweck, Deal, September 21, 1986.

6. Ibid.

7. Ibid.

8. Interview with David Sitton, Jerusalem, May 8, 1986.

9. Edward Grossman, "Where the Melting-Pot Failed," *Jerusalem Post Magazine* (May 30, 1986): 8.

10. Interview with Moishe Cohen, Tel Aviv, May 15, 1986. Virtually the same conclusion was reached by Menachem Yedid, chairman of the Israel Council for Rescue of Jews from Arab Lands. Speaking before the second international conference of the World Organization of Jews from Arab Countries in London in November, 1983, Yedid quoted sources of the Cyprus-based *Middle East Times* that suggested most Syrian Jews would leave if given the opportunity.

11. Ora Schweitzer, "WOJAC Raises Plight of Syrian Jewish Women in Nairobi," *WOJAC* 2 (January-February 1986):5.

12. Cohen interview, May 15, 1986.

13. Shalom interview, September 23, 1986. In 1988 the Lahti family was permitted to emigrate from Syria.

14. Telephone interview with Judy Feld Carr, June 27, 1985.

15. Telephone interview with Judy Feld Carr, September 26, 1986.

16. Letter, Jewish correspondent in Syria, September 11, 1986.

17. Interview with Jeanette Cattan, New York, September, 24, 1986.

18. Interview with Miriam Meyouchas, Jerusalem, April 13, 1986.

19. "Interview with Dr. Ruth Feur," *The Battle* 1 (February 1986):12–13.

20. Sitton interview, May 8, 1986.

21. *Misgav Yerushalayim* was founded by Elie Eliachar, president of the Sephardic community in Jerusalem for more than thirty years and a member of the Knesset from 1949 to 1955. Currently it is undertaking a survey of the Eliachar family archive, which

dates back to the end of the fifteenth century, in anticipation of the 1992 anniversary of the expulsion of Jews from Spain. At some meetings, Ladino is still spoken.

22. Sitton interview, May 8, 1986.

23. *Cleveland Plain Dealer*, Nov. 1, 1987, sect. A, p. 8.

24. Shalom interview, September 23, 1986.

25. Ibid.

26. Cohen interview, May 8, 1986.

27. Interview with Sherry Hyman, Joint Distribution Committee, New York, September 23, 1986.

28. Saleh Mukamal, report to Canadian Jewish Congress on the World Organization of Jews from Arab Countries Conference, Washington, D.C., October 26–29, 1987, pp. 2–3. An earlier interview with a representative of the Israeli Foreign Office, Jerusalem, May 20, 1986 elicited the comment that officially Israel could not have any public position on the question of Jewish refugees from Arab lands.

29. Cohen interview, May 8, 1986.

30. Those interested in offering assistance should consider contacting the Ronald Feld Fund for Jews from Arab Lands, Beth Tzedec Congregation, 1700 Bathurst Street, Toronto, Canada M5P 3K3; the Ronald Feld Fund of Beth Tefiloh, 3300 Old Court Rd., Baltimore, Maryland 21208; the Women's Association for Neighbourhood Activities in Jerusalem c/o the Sephardic Studies Program, Yeshiva University, 500 West 185th Street, New York, New York 10033; The World Organization of Jews from Arab Countries, 118a Ben Yehuda Street, Tel Aviv, Israel; or the Joint Distribution Committee, 711 3rd Avenue, New York, New York 10017.

31. On Russian television, Chirac noted that it was "extraordinary" that only two countries (Syria and the Soviet Union) blocked emigration of Jews. *Canadian Jewish News* (July 23, 1987):7.

32. Leib Olitski, "My Song to the Jewish People," in *A Treasury of Jewish Poetry*, Nathan and Marynn Ausubel, eds. (New York: Crown, 1957), p. 185.

Postscript

1. As related to the author at a meeting in Cleveland of the Jewish Community Relations Council's representatives, February 5, 1989.

2. As related to the author by a Canadian source.

3. Ibid.

Bibliographic Essay

Several years ago, Edward Said, the Palestinian semanticist, assessed the mass of literature dealing with the Middle East and found it wanting. Histories, memoirs, travelogues, gazeteers and guidebooks published in the West since 1800 were, he said, permeated with "Orientalism," a condescension rooted in racism. The creation of Arab Studies centers at prestigious institutions like Georgetown, The University of Texas at Austin, and Columbia University through endowments supplied by oil companies and/or petroleum-exporting nations, apparently has rectified that situation; for now, the student researching the Middle East not only has access to a range of texts favorable to Islamic culture, but also those which distort history, like Philip Mattar's *The Mufti of Jerusalem*, hailed as a "sensitive and sensible" study of Haj Amin el-Husseini.

Unfortunately, there has been no comparable profusion of literature dealing with the status of Jews in Arab lands. With the exception of the excellent study by Joan Peters, most of the works cited in the text (Joseph B. Schechtman, S. D. Goitein, Itzhak Ben-Zvi) are more than twenty-five years old. Several (A. Chouraqui and A. Memmi) are personal pleas for understanding that have fallen on deaf ears since the mid–1970s. Only Bat Ye'Or, Norman Stillman, and Bernard Lewis have addressed the issue of Arab anti-Semitism, favoring, for the most part, a generalized approach. There are a few other books worthy of note, such as Dafna Alon, *Arab Racialism* (Jerusalem: Israel Economist, 1969); Hayim Cohen, *The Jews of the Middle East, 1860–1972* (New York: Wiley, 1973); Devora and Menahem Hacohen, *One People: The Story of Eastern Jews* (New York: Funk and Wagnalls, 1969); Nehemiah Robinson, *The Arab Countries of the Near East and Their Jewish Communities* (New York: Institute of Jewish Affairs, 1951), and several reports, including David Littman, *Protected Peoples Under Islam* (Jerusalem: Bat Ye'or, 1976); Mordecai Nisan, *Human Rights in the Arab Countries* (New York: Middle East Review, Special Studies, 1981); and Maurice Roumani, *The Case of the Jews from Arab*

Countries: A Neglected Issue (Jerusalem: World Organization of Jews from Arab Countries, 1983).

Occasionally, and only in recent years, books dealing with the status of Jews in specific Middle Eastern countries have appeared. These include Renzo De Felice, *Jews in an Arab Land: Libya: 1835–1870*, trans. Judith Roumani (Austin: University of Texas, 1985); Jacob Mann, *The Jews in Egypt and in Palestine under the Fatimid Caliphs*, ed. S. D. Goitein (New York: Ktav, 1970); Moshe Ma'oz, ed., *Sources for History of Jews in Syria and Israel in the 19th Century* (Jerusalem: Hebrew University, 1971); and Aryeh Shmuelevitz, *The Jews of the Ottoman Empire in the Late 15th and 16th Centuries* (Leiden: E. J. Brill, 1984). It is significant that each of these is a "safe" study of a Jewish community chronologically removed from the current hostilities in the Middle East.

Nissam Rejwan, has addressed the persecution of one group in *The Jews of Iraq: 3000 Years of History and Culture* (Boulder: Westview, 1985). But just as in medieval times, scarcity of information and fear for the welfare of Jews in Iran or Syria have veiled their agony. Researchers interested in the plight of Syrian Jewry may consult the works of Anne Sinai and Allen Pollack, eds., *The Syrian Arab Republic* (New York: American Professors for Peace in the Middle East, 1976); *The Plight of Syrian Jewry* (Paris: International Conference for the Deliverance of Jews in the Middle East, 1974); *Syria: A Prison to 4500 Jews* (Toronto: Committee for Jews in Arab Lands, 1974); and the excellent essay by Oded Tavor, "Syria," *Encyclopedia Judaica* 15 (Jerusalem: Keter, 1971), 636–49. Joseph Sutton in Brooklyn should also be saluted for his efforts at recounting the Syrian Jewish adaptation to America in *Magic Carpet: Aleppo in Flatbush* (New York: Thayer-Jacoby, 1980) and *Aleppo Chronicles: The Story of the Unique Sepharadeem of the Ancient Near East* (New York: Thayer-Jacoby, 1988). Apart from these, there are unpublished theses and the passing fancies of journals.

In the wake of the Six Day War of June, 1967, the London-based *Jewish Observer* made the torture of Jewish prisoners in Syrian jails a priority. In the next five years, the *Observer* published a score of articles detailing the murder of fifty-seven Syrian Jews (July 7, 1967), outlining conditions in the Mazza jail (October 28, 1971), quoting appeals from non sectarian groups (October 8, 1971), and calling for a U.N. investigation of Syrian human rights violations (August 9, 1968, a move quashed by the Secretary General U Thant). Similar concern was voiced by I. L. Kenen's *Near East Report* (November 26, 1976; March 24, 1976; February 28, 1979); the American Jewish Congress' *Congress Monthly* (September, 1975; April, 1976); *The Israel Digest* (October 20, 1967; April 4, 1969; October 29, 1971); and *Jewish Digest* (February, 1976; September, 1977; November, 1977). Most of these articles, however, were cryptic, single-page affairs, sometimes subsumed under the title of world news. Longer essays like I. B. Yaakov's, "The Jewish Remnant in Arab Lands—Can They Be Saved?" *American Zionist* 59 (April 1969), 33–34; R. Bashan's, "Jews Plight in Arab Countries," *Israel* 1, no. 9 (1968), 5–8; S. Friedman's, "Crack of Doom Hangs over Jews in the Middle East," *Chronicle Review* (May-June, 1972); W. P. Zenner's, "Syrian Jews in Three Social Settings," *Jewish Journal of Sociology* 10 (June 1968), 101–120; and, J. Kimche's "Syria Without Assad?" *Midstream* (June/July 1985), 3–5, coming as they did from Jewish sources, were greeted skeptically, especially after 1975 when the Assad government made a concerted effort to improve its image with the West and the airing of a "60 Minutes" episode.

International rescue committees come and go—just as editors do—the victims of egos and shifting priorities. General Clay's committee that listed a formidable lineup of politicians and entertainers is no more. The Israel Rescue Committee apparently is in disarray. Yet somehow, this very year, the Union of American Hebrew Congregations (Reform Judaism) has adopted the issue of Syrian Jewry for the first time, urging Jewish community relations groups to work for their human rights and circulating a fact sheet that is in some parts eighteen years old.

Only one organization in the United States has maintained a vigilant watch on the status of Jews in Syria and the entire Middle East, and that is the American Jewish Committee. The releases and articles of Dr. George Gruen in *Present Tense*, *Hadassah* and *Na'amat Woman* have been the most reliable sources of information on these problems. Ultimately, however, even Dr. Gruen defers to the Canadian Committee for Jews in Arab Lands and its extraordinary leader, Judy Feld Carr.

Index

About the Author

SAUL S. FRIEDMAN is a Professor of History at Youngstown State University, Youngstown, Ohio. He is the author of *Land of Dust: Palestine at the Turn of the Century* (1982), *No Haven for the Oppressed: United States Policy Toward Jewish Refugees, 1938–1945* (1973); *The Oberammergau Passion Play: A Lance Against Civilization* (1984); and *Pogromchik: The Assassination of Simon Petlura* (1976).